ASK A
MEDIUM

About the Author

Spiritualist minister Rose Vanden Eynden earned her mediumship credentials in 2000 after four years of study. That same year, she founded the United Spiritualists of the Christ Light Church (USCL) in Cincinnati, Ohio, where she serves as a minister and instructor. She conducts personal readings, group sessions, and workshops across the country and in her private practice. This is her third book. Please visit her online at www.vandeneynden.biz.

ASK A
MEDIUM

Answers to

Your Frequently

Asked Questions

About the

Spirit World

Rose Vanden Eynden

Llewellyn Publications
Woodbury, Minnesota

First Edition
First Printing, 2010

Cover art: window image © LushPix/Unlisted Images, Inc.
Cover design by Kevin R. Brown
Editing by Brett Fechheimer
Llewellyn is a registered trademark of Llewellyn Worldwide, Ltd.

Library of Congress Cataloging-in-Publication Data
Vanden Eynden, Rose.
  Ask a medium : answers to your frequently asked questions about the
spirit world / Rose Vanden Eynden.—1st ed.
      p. cm.
  Includes bibliographical references.
  ISBN 978-0-7387-1898-9
  1. Mediums. I. Title.
  BF1286.V35 2010
  133.9'1—dc22
                          2009032204

Llewellyn Worldwide does not participate in, endorse, or have any authority or
responsibility concerning private business transactions between our authors and the
public.
  All mail addressed to the author is forwarded but the publisher cannot, unless specifically instructed by the author, give out an address or phone number.
  Any Internet references contained in this work are current at publication time,
but the publisher cannot guarantee that a specific location will continue to be maintained. Please refer to the publisher's website for links to authors' websites and other
sources.

Llewellyn Publications
A Division of Llewellyn Worldwide, Ltd.
2143 Wooddale Drive, Dept. 978-0-7387-1898-9
Woodbury, Minnesota 55125-2989, U.S.A.
www.llewellyn.com

Printed in the United States of America

Other books by Rose Vanden Eynden

So You Want to Be a Medium? A Down-to-Earth Guide
(Also available in Spanish as *¿Quieres Ser Medium?*)

Metatron: Invoking the Angel of God's Presence

For my sons, Max and Ben, who teach me new things every day.
May you find the answers to every question you ask,
and may you never question how very loved you are.

CONTENTS

INTRODUCTION

Life's greatest journeys begin with questions.

I remember my older brother clambering aboard a big yellow bus to take him to school, while my mother and I watched from the driveway. "Why can't I go with Mike?" I asked, tugging at my mother's hand.

"Because you're not old enough yet," she replied patiently.

The bus lumbered up the street, a puff of exhaust trailing behind. "But I wanna go. Why ain't I old enough?"

"Why *aren't* I old enough," my mother corrected. "When you go to school, they'll teach you to talk good." She smiled, although I didn't get the joke then. When I finally arrived at school a few years later, I fell in love with learning. It became a lifelong passion—and, I was allowed to ride that big yellow school bus, too.

Many years later, another question: what college are you attending? My choice brought me hours of fervent study; incredible memories of projects, shows, and achievements; and friendships that I cherish even today.

Flash forward a few more years: my boyfriend on one knee in the living room of my parents' home, his hand outstretched to take mine as he pops that question most girls dream about from the time they're tiny princesses. The engagement ring he slips on my finger seals our bond a year before we take our marriage vows in a church packed with people. Nearly two decades later, we're still going strong.

And a perfect circle: my own twin sons sitting on my lap, pacifiers in their mouths, pointing at images in a picture book. "Dat?" they ask, and I answer: "Cat." "Dog." "Fish." "Ball." "Baby." I squeeze them tightly to me, the book balanced between us all, trying to freeze the moment in time.

It doesn't work, of course. They continue to grow older, and wiser, and I continue to answer their questions as best I can, just like my mother did for me.

Still another of my greatest life journeys began with a question posed by a friend: "Do you want to come to a psychic-development class at my house?" I'd been reading Tarot cards for years by then, but I wanted to continue to learn and grow. I wanted my spiritual path to infuse every aspect of my life, not just one area of it. Going to that class, and the incredible odyssey that began there, helped to bring that intention into manifested reality.

After years of diligent study in a Spiritualist seminary program, I was tested by a panel of experienced mediums and proved my ability to contact the spirit world. I became a certified, professional medium, adding to my skills as a Tarot reader and psychic. Each year, I conduct hundreds of personal readings and group sittings where I connect with people who have passed to the Other Side and wish to communicate from there with their loved ones here on the physical plane.

I also chose to become an ordained Spiritualist minister, and I served a church community for several years as Assistant Pastor and Director of Education. During my tenure, I designed an intensive mediumship training program for those who wished to study after-death communication, which produced over a dozen excellent mediums who now use those skills professionally. After working with students in this capacity, I began to think about people who might want to make their own connections to Spirit but didn't have the opportunity to study with an institution like our church or the place I attended seminary.

My first book, *So You Want to Be a Medium? A Down-to-Earth Guide*, was born from the desire to communicate with a larger audience hungry to get in touch with Spirit themselves. My second book, *Metatron: Invoking the Angel of God's Presence*, grew from my experiences of working with that specific archangel and the myriad questions I'd had about angels and their special energies. Every year, I use my education degree to teach as many classes as I can on a variety of metaphysical topics, including mediumship development and other subjects addressing contact with the spirit world. I've hosted a spiritual radio show in my hometown of Cincinnati, Ohio, and I've been featured on many other programs, speaking extensively about after-death communication and spirit contact. I feel blessed, because I believe I've found my purpose in life: to bring information from the spirit world to those that wish to learn more about it.

In the years I've been a practicing clairvoyant and a mediumship-development teacher, I've fielded countless questions from anxious seekers eager to understand the spirit world. My clients and students come from across the economic, political, and social spectrum. Through my work I've met teachers, scientists, blue-collar workers, healers, religious leaders, artists, stay-at-home parents, architects, students, engineers, salespeople, journalists, and many others.

Even though these folks come from very different backgrounds and lead unique lives, their questions are remarkably similar. Many are personal ("Is my dad doing OK on the Other Side?"), but more are general inquiries regarding the nature of spirit communication, what souls are doing once they make their transition to the Other Side, how the afterlife looks, what really happens to a soul during the death process, and other similar matters. After hearing the same questions over and over again from individual sitters and from groups for whom I've read or taught, I decided to start a list of questions, with the intention of collecting them into a source where I could record the answers I'd found through research and through information obtained from those speaking from the Other Side. All of the questions in this book come from that list, and the answers reflect the explanations I've gathered from many different sources.

A particular question, though, haunts my thoughts like some people believe ghosts haunt old buildings (a topic we'll discuss in greater detail later). This question was put to me at a lecture I gave at a local psychic festival. This event, an extremely popular affair showcasing metaphysical vendors, readers, and healers, attracted a large crowd that weekend. My lecture hall was stuffed with listeners. They seated themselves on the floor around me when the all the chairs were taken; they leaned against the walls and stood outside the single doorway, trying to hear. I'd spent most of my fifty minutes talking about spirit communication and how it works, and I was fielding questions from the audience. A hand in the back of the room waved, and I called on that woman, pacing down the aisle so I could hear her better.

She was about my age, maybe a few years younger, with dark hair and a tense, furrowed brow that made her appear angry. "You sure sound like you know what you're talking about," she said in a clear, carrying voice. "But how do you know you're right?"

The question stopped me in my tracks. "I'm . . . I'm sorry?" I stuttered, not quite sure what she was asking.

"Spirit guides. The afterlife. What it's all like. How do you know you're right?" She shrugged. "You could say anything you wanted. How do you know you're right?"

I've carried that question with me ever since as inspiration to do the best work I can. In my mediumship practice, I've conducted countless readings for sitters during which spirits have come through and explained, described, and recounted their experiences with the death transition, what the Other

Side is like, what souls do when they get there, why they can or cannot communicate, and innumerable other subjects. I've spent untold hours researching similar topics in libraries, books, classes, online, and through interviews with friends, church members, and acquaintances, trying to make sense of all the information available about these fascinating mysteries. What I've discovered as truth, I've compiled into this book. I've tried my best to pass on to you, the reader, the best answers I can find about the hows, whys, and wherefores of spirit work.

Even so, secrets still remain. The great scientist Albert Einstein said, "The most beautiful thing we can experience is the mysterious. It is the source of all true art and science. He to whom this emotion is a stranger, who can no longer pause to wonder and stand rapt in awe, is as good as dead: his eyes are closed." In this statement, Einstein cuts to the heart of the matter: there will always be mysteries in the Universe, and the world of Spirit, as you'll see from this book, is filled with hidden knowledge. Since the beginning of time, human beings have wondered what happens when we die, if an afterlife exists, and hundreds of other questions revolving around our connection to Divinity and our place in Its grand scheme. Celebrated philosophers have pondered these questions and spun theories, and noteworthy scholars have explored the frontiers of science to probe for explanations. Their work has been preserved, and it still continues, as I hope to illustrate here.

And yet we still don't know all the answers. In my mind the best response seems to be the one I gave to the questioning woman that day at the lecture:

I can only tell you about my experience. I can only share with you what I've discovered that has fit with my own sensibilities and understanding. And I can only hope that you'll take these answers, explore them on your own, see how they fit with your experiences and philosophy, and find out for yourself if they resonate as truth.

And perhaps, with this book, I can do one other thing. Maybe I can inspire you to keep looking. If a response to a question here doesn't make sense to you, or seems incomplete in some way, maybe it's an indication that more work and more investigation needs to be done in that particular area of interest. And maybe, just maybe, you're the person to take up that challenge.

So, my friends, we'll embark on our journey in this book together. I'll show you what I know of the spirit world and its inner workings, and I'll explain to the best of my ability the information that's been revealed to me. I'll cite sources when I can so that you can consult those, and possibly others, as you work to gather details for your enlightenment. I'll endeavor to share with you what I've learned by answering questions gathered from people just like you, who have come to me for readings to connect them to their dead relatives and their spirit teachers—folks who have attended my mediumship development classes and workshops, striving to understand their own unique abilities and their own connections to Spirit. These questions will most assuredly take you on an amazing and illuminating personal journey.

Great Creator, You Who are the Source of all knowledge, all wisdom, and all mystery, please bless these pages and fill them with Your instructive Light. Open our eyes, our minds, and our hearts to understand our places in Your Divine Plan, and allow us to comprehend how best we may serve that agenda. Enlighten us so that we may feel closer to You, and strengthen our relationships with all of Your creations. In the holiest name we pray, amen.

BASICS: THE FOUNDATIONS OF SPIRIT

I was born, raised, and have lived most of my life in Cincinnati, Ohio. If you've never had the pleasure of visiting my beautiful hometown, then you've probably never sampled Cincinnati-style chili (seasoned with chocolate, served over cooked spaghetti, and topped with chopped onions and mounds of grated cheddar cheese), wouldn't understand the battle between the East Side and West Side of our town, and might be baffled to hear just-introduced strangers inquiring about which high school the other attended over twenty years ago.

As in all cities, certain things make Cincinnati unique. One that puzzles most visitors to no end is our use of the word *please*. To a native Cincinnatian, *please* is a polite way to ask for compliance from someone else, and we were taught by our parents to use it just as everyone else does: "Please pass the salt." "Can I please go with Molly to the movies on Saturday?" But we also say *please* to mean "pardon me" or "excuse me," especially if we misunderstand or can't hear the request that the other party has made. Until I went to college, I had no idea that this use of the word *please* was foreign to anyone living outside of our city.

My freshman roommate was from Pennsylvania, and we'd only shared a room for a few days when she came in one evening, turned around, and presented her back to me. She held up her hair to expose her neck, along with an open zipper that snaked all the way down the back of her dress. I blinked in surprise, still lost in the textbook I'd been reading, as she murmured a request that I couldn't quite hear. "Please?" I responded automatically, my brain still not understanding what she wanted. Sighing loudly, she rolled her eyes and said, "Will you zip me up, *please*?"

I laugh about that situation now, because it took me several minutes to convince my roommate that I wasn't criticizing her manners. As a native Cincinnatian, I was asking her to repeat herself because I hadn't heard her first question. This story is a good example of how the use of certain words and phrases hold different meanings for different people. Over the course of my life, I've seen many more examples of how people trying to communicate with each other can become completely confused about the message the other is trying to impart because they misunderstand the words the other person is using. This difference in semantics can break down the entire conversation and sometimes leave the participants feeling angry and frustrated unless someone recognizes when it's happening.

For this reason, I want to begin with some very basic questions and answers that define the words we'll be using in this book. As a teacher, I like each of my students to use the same semantics when talking about spiritual subjects. This helps us all to better understand our fellow students, our instructors, and ultimately, ourselves. With this in mind, let's look at some simple questions that will help us all to start with the same spiritual foundation. Please.

What is a psychic? What is a medium? Is there a difference?

Yes, there is a difference between a psychic and a medium. A psychic receives impressions about a client's past, present, and future by using extrasensory perception or telepathy. Extrasensory perception relies on input from forces outside of a human being's normal five senses (sight, hearing, smell, taste, and touch) and is not based on rational deduction from information the psychic already possesses. Telepathy allows a psychic to access the client's mind, thus providing an accurate measure of the situations occurring in the client's life and the client's feelings concerning them. In contrast, a medium receives information through direct contact with the spirit world and the entities that reside there, including angels, spirit guides, teachers, masters, and deceased loved ones. In communication with people who have died, a medium must relay evidential messages from these passed loved ones, thus proving that life continues on in the spirit world and contact with these energies does not cease after death. All mediums are psychic, but not all psychics are mediums.

You mentioned angels, spirit guides, teachers, and masters that reside in the spirit world along with our deceased loved ones. Who are they?

Spirit guides, teachers, and masters are entities that usually had a physical incarnation at some point in history and now reside as energy beings in the spirit world. Besides working to achieve their own highest spiritual progressions, their main purposes are to help the souls here in the physical world by working with them individually or en masse on their own quests for soul advancement. They share their knowledge, wisdom, and guidance with us through spirit communication. Angels are a completely separate entity created by the Divine to be helpers to humanity. They are not human, but their main purpose is to serve humanity as protectors, helpmates, and positive, guiding influences. We'll talk more about the specifics of all of these spiritual energies in the chapter entitled "Spirit Guides, Teachers, and Angels."

Where is the spirit world?

The spirit world interpenetrates the physical world in which we dwell. It surrounds us and intermingles in every way with our existence, even if we're completely unaware of its presence. Science tells us that everything in the Universe vibrates; that is, the molecules of matter are in constant motion. Some things vibrate at a faster, or higher, rate than others. The entities residing in the spirit world vibrate at a much faster and higher rate than we do, which is why we can't always see or feel the spirit world and its inhabitants around us. Many of us, though, have caught a glimpse of the spirit world out of the corner of our eye. Have you ever had the experience of seeing a flash of movement or a sparkle in the air next to you, but when you turn to look, it's gone? You've just seen a spirit move past you! Your eye caught the higher and faster vibration for a split second, but our eyes cannot always see this movement, much like we can't see the propeller on an airplane when it's spinning rapidly as it readies for take-off. Have you ever heard your name called aloud, but when you've turned to see who was addressing you, the room was empty? This is another example of experiencing the unseen spirit world that is in constant motion all around our own physical world. Our deceased loved ones haven't left us when they cross over to the Other Side; we may not be able to see or touch them, but their vibrations are much more accessible and much closer than most of us think.

You keep using the word *spirit*. What is a spirit? What is a ghost? Are they the same thing?

Spirits and ghosts are similar, but they are not the same. Both spirits and ghosts are the energy components of a physical human experience—what remains when the human body dies. Thanks to the incredible work of talented scientists, we know that energy can be neither created nor destroyed. The body may shut down, give out, and stop working, but the energy, the essence, of a human being has to go somewhere. This energy continues on as either a spirit or a ghost. When someone dies, his essence, or soul energy, makes the transition to the spirit world, where he will continue to grow as a spiritual being. We thus say that this loved one is now a spirit on the Other Side. When someone dies, however, but does not accept that her soul essence has left her physical body and she is now pure energy, this loved one becomes a ghost. A ghost does not completely make her transition to the Other Side because she does not accept the new condition of her existence. Until she accepts this and moves into the loving light that awaits her in the spirit world, she will remain a ghost.

Ghosts are very attracted to the physical world and will often take up residence in a place that was special to them during their lifetime. The important thing to remember in these instances is that ghosts are not trapped. They can embrace their new reality at any time and complete their transition to the spirit world. There is a constant pull toward the loving light of the world of Spirit, but a ghost resists this, refusing to accept the reality of her departure from the physical body.

Some ghosts "haunt" houses, museums, landmarks, and other places special to them, hoping somehow to reclaim their physical existence. This is not the way to be reborn, however, which we'll discover when we discuss the reincarnation process in the chapter entitled "Reincarnation and Other Lifetimes." Because some ghosts are upset by or irritated with their new existence, they become noisy or disruptive, which can get the attention of people still in a physical body in close proximity to them. Most ghosts, however, are not dangerous, and some mediums work at helping ghosts to realize the reality of their new energy by encouraging the ghosts to move into the light of the spirit world to embrace the next step of their spiritual progression.

Just as a note: *spirit* spelled with a lowercase *s* refers to an individual soul, or it is used as a descriptor, as in "the spirit world." When Spirit is spelled with a capital *S*, it refers to the larger spirit universe, including all guides, teachers, deceased loved ones, angels, and other spiritual entities, while also implying a belief in a Divine Source (God) Who created it all.

So is there a difference between a spirit and a soul?

The difference here lies in how most people think about these two terms. The soul is often defined as the spiritual essence of a human being, the part of us that continues on after death in a place called heaven, the afterlife, the Other Side, and so forth. We often think about the soul as the spiritual side of a human being, but we don't consider the soul to be an energy with which we can commune and communicate. Although the soul is what continues on after death, we use the word *spirit* instead, which seems to imply more "human" characteristics. We can see a spirit with our eyes, we can hear a spirit's voice, we can feel the touch of a spirit—but we don't use the word *soul* interchangeably here. It's really a matter of semantics, for the soul and the spirit are the same thing.

Can all spirits communicate from the Other Side?

Yes, they all can, but they may choose not to for various reasons. Sometimes, when a soul first makes the transition to the spirit world, he may have other activities demanding his attention (which we'll learn more about in the chapter entitled

"The Other Side"), and he may not be able to communicate right away. Some souls may need to relearn the process of communication once they've reached the Other Side. And just like here in the physical world, spirits are occupied with various jobs, hobbies, and events in the afterlife, which may impinge on the amount of time and energy they can spend communicating with our world. When a spirit is not communicating, it could be because he is relearning the communication process, he is busy doing something else, or he is simply exercising his free will and choosing not to communicate at that particular moment. Most of the time, however, our spirit loved ones want very much to communicate with us, so don't take it personally if and when they're not available.

Can all people here in the physical world communicate with those in the spirit world?

Yes! Every person is able to communicate with spirit guides, angels, and deceased loved ones. This is an inherent skill in all people, although it may be easier for some than for others. With the exception of those born with disabilities, we all come into this world with our five physical senses: sight, hearing, taste, touch, and smell. We are also born with an exceptional nonphysical aptitude that is sometimes called our *sixth sense*, and this extrasensory capacity includes our psychic perceptions and our ability to communicate with Spirit.

Just as we relate to the physical world through our five senses, we can also learn to relate to the spirit world through our psychic senses. These lie dormant in many of us because our society does not encourage the use of these skills. For some people, the ability to see, hear, or understand Spirit is always prevalent; many professional psychics and mediums relate stories of their encounters with dead relatives or their spirit guides from the earliest times they can remember. I myself recall many instances from my childhood of precognition and dreams that came true. But everyone, even those who have never had an experience with psychic energy, can learn how to access the intuitive side of the brain and open up the psychic receptors to receive and understand spirit messages.

Just as we can all learn to play soccer or to bake a fancy dessert, we can all learn how to communicate with the spirit world. And, just to be clear: folks with disabilities are mediums, too. Spirit uses many different methods to relay messages to those open to receive them. Just because you can't see in the physical world doesn't mean you won't be able to perceive Spirit in your mind's eye. Spirit communication is another way in which all humanity is equal and blessed by Creator, because we all have the ability to receive the guidance and wisdom that is offered to us through Spirit's intercession.

Now that we're all working from a shared concept of Spirit, we can begin to explore in detail the spirit world and those that dwell within it. Let's start by meeting some of the energies that inhabit the spirit planes—they're perfect tour guides, and are more than willing to share their understanding of the inner workings of the Other Side. Follow me as I make the introductions.

Spirit Guides, Teachers, and Angels

One of my greatest loves in life is the theatre. I performed in my first play at the age of thirteen, and the incredible euphoria I enjoyed from that experience drove me to audition for musicals during my high-school years and to pursue a degree in theatre education in college. There's something almost intoxicating about live performance, whether you're the one in the spotlight or you're watching from off-stage or from your seat in the audience. When my husband took me to New York City for my fortieth birthday and I finally saw my first Broadway show, I nearly wept from excitement before the play had even started.

Those who have never been involved in the theatre really have no idea of how complex a process a live production can be. As audience members, we see the actors on stage, and we may see a stagehand dressed all in black scurry across the set during a scene change, but it's easy to forget about all the others who make a show come to life. I've had many acting roles on stage, but I've also been a stage manager, a director, a lighting technician, a sound technician, a props master, and a costume runner behind the scenes of different productions. Having served in all these positions, I can honestly say that putting together a show is one of the hardest and most complicated projects I've ever undertaken. It's also one of the most rewarding. It must be—I keep doing it, and I don't intend to ever stop. (And from what I understand of the Other Side, I won't have to—there's theatre there, too. We'll talk more about that later.)

With so many people executing so many tasks, the theatre is a true team experience. Obviously, without the lighting designer to position the lamps and the lighting technician to execute the cues, the actors would stumble around in the dark. If the actors decided to simply improvise on stage instead of performing their rehearsed lines, who knows what might happen during a show? Even the management staff of a production is important; taking care of the audience members is key to a successful performance. Without every member of the team trying his or her best to achieve quality results, a theatre production could turn into an absurd fiasco.

The feeling of being a part of a dedicated team like this is amazing, and I've noticed it inspires me to give every ounce of energy I possibly can whenever I'm lucky enough to be involved in a show. Every other member of the team is working diligently to mount the very best production possible, and as a part of that, you can't possibly give any less. Sharing in that driven energy is as rewarding as the opening of the show itself.

If you've never had this experience in the theatre, you can have a similar one in your life, and you don't even have to leave your own home to do so. You have a team of amazing experts with you right now, whether you're aware of them or not. Working together, you can achieve the awesome goal of advancing as a spiritual soul. All you need to do is recognize and interact with your band of spirit guides, teachers, and angels. By making your spiritual progression a priority in your life, you'll forge ahead toward the enlightenment every soul is yearning to attain. You can also work with your spirit helpers to accomplish goals and attain great joy during your earthly existence—and who doesn't want more of that?

In this chapter, we'll discuss who spirit guides, teachers, and angels are, and how these loving entities can help you with many aspects of your life and your work as a soul. Get comfortable, because we've got a lot of information to cover!

What is a spirit guide?

As mentioned earlier, a spirit guide is an entity that usually had a physical incarnation at some point in the past but whose personality and soul now reside as pure energy in the spirit world. We acquire our spirit guides (and yes, we all have more than one) through the Natural Law of Attraction, which dictates that like energy attracts like energy. Just as we tend to make friends with those people who have similar hobbies as ours during our lifetimes, we attract spirit guides who have corresponding personalities and interests to journey with us through our life challenges and goals. These spirit guides agree to be with us before we enter the physical body; we meet with them and make agreements with them while still pure energy ourselves on the Other Side.

When we incarnate into a physical body on the earth plane, our spirit guides stay close to us, ready at all times to assist us when we need their help. Unfortunately, many of us do not realize the aid that is available to us through our spirit guides, and we do not utilize their expertise and their skills when we could. It's important to realize that our spirit guides love us and want to help us, but they cannot do anything for us if we haven't given them permission to do so. Our spirit guides recognize the importance of free will, one of the greatest gifts given to us by Creator, and they will never interfere in ours. This is why we must ask them for help and guidance. They will not impose on our free will if we haven't asked.

So spirit guides were once alive?

Technically, spirit guides are *still* alive—they've just transformed to pure energy forms, a transition that we call death. Most spirit guides have had at least one physical lifetime on Earth, and many have had more than one lifetime. Some people who take the time to get to know their spirit guides come to understand that they've shared a previous lifetime with one or more of their guides. This may partly explain why certain guides are with us—we may recognize each other from previous lifetimes together on a soul level and want to work with each other again. Spirit guides can help those with whom they're working to understand their past-life experiences together and what lessons from those lifetimes their souls did or did not learn. This is one thing that makes spirit guides so helpful to us: they have had life experiences themselves on Earth, and they can advise us based on that knowledge as well as the wealth of wisdom available now to them in the spirit planes.

What's the difference between a spirit guide and a spirit teacher?

As I mentioned, we have more than one spirit guide working with us during our lifetime. Most of us have at least five, possibly more, depending on our life's work and the goals we are trying to accomplish. Since we have several guides working with us, we may think of them as "specialists" in certain areas of our life. For instance, we have a joy guide, who concentrates her energies on helping us to stay positive, happy, and focused. Our protector guide works with us on issues of dispelling negative energy and keeping us physically safe. An artist may have a guide that helps with her creations, and a counselor may have a guide that aids him in listening to clients with a more attentive ear. Spirit teachers are guides that are even more specialized; they are present with every person in an attempt to help their charges in issues of morality, ethics, and spiritual matters.

Sometimes the terms *spirit guide* and *spirit teacher* are used interchangeably, and it is important to note that all of our guides want to share their knowledge, wisdom, and love with us. The terms used don't really matter; cultivating a relationship with them is the important task.

What about angels? Are they the same as spirit guides or spirit teachers?

No. Angels are a completely separate energy, created by the Divine for a specific purpose. This purpose—to help humanity—is similar to the task that spirit guides have taken on, so it is understandable that we sometimes confuse the two groups of energies. Spirit teachers choose the path of guidance to achieve more in their own personal soul development. As they are able to help us, they progress spiritually on the Other Side. Angels, however, are commissioned to be of service to humanity and to all of the inhabitants of the many worlds, both seen and unseen, that God created. Angels have a very high-energy vibration and are attracted by loving, pure thoughts and actions. Just as we can learn to connect with our spirit guides and teachers, we can also learn how to communicate with angels. They are an important part of the spirit world, and they are wonderful allies that can truly help us to learn, change, and grow.

What are elementals and totems? Can we have these as spirit guides?

Elementals are energies that exist in the natural kingdoms of the earth plane, caring for and influencing these habitats and environments. Probably the best known of the elementals are the faeries, which are associated with the element of air. Faeries are beautiful, small, winged creatures that can and do interact with human beings. They are thought to be mischievous and highly intelligent, and they usually enjoy living outdoors in the fresh air as opposed to dwelling in stuffy houses.

Undines are elementals associated with water. In literature, they are often called mermaids or mermen, and they are depicted as having human bodies and fish-like tails. They dwell in all waterways and care very deeply for the animals and other living creatures that share this environment.

Gnomes are the elementals associated with the earth and its stewardship. They are thought to live deep underground or in caves, appearing as dark, hairy creatures with a great passion for protecting their homes and their race.

Finally, salamanders are the elementals associated with fire. Like their physical counterparts, they appear to be lizard-like creatures that dwell in hot areas, especially deserts and all places where fires burn. They have temperaments to match their blazing environments, and they are shrewd and smart influences in the natural world.

Elementals can and do take on the role of spirit guides for some people. Faeries seem to be the group most willing to work with human beings in this capacity, although I know one dear lady who has a gnome for a spirit guide. Remember: in the case of spirit guides, like attracts like; you may have an elemental spirit guide because of your own affinity for the natural world or your dedication to protecting and nurturing the environment. Whatever the reason, getting to know an elemental spirit guide is similar to connecting with a human one. We'll talk more about that process in just a little while.

In some Native American traditions, a totem is an animal energy that can be the symbol for a person, tribe, or family. These totem animals act as spirit guides for the people to whom they are connected, offering protection, power, and wisdom just as human spirit guides do. A totem animal also has a specific medicine, or energy, connected to it, which the person may need at particular times in his life. For example, one of my totem animals is dog, which represents faith, loyalty, guidance, and teaching. These are all attributes and areas that I have had challenges and successes with over the years.

If you feel drawn to a specific animal, or if you dream about an animal or seem to have a certain animal appear in your life quite often, chances are that this is one of your totems. You may have one or several, and different totems may become more or less prevalent at different times of your life. Totem animals have great wisdom to share with us, and they are another guiding force for us if we choose to learn to listen.

How can I get to know my spirit guides?

One of the most important things to understand about your spirit guides is that they *want* to work with you. They want the communication process to be as easy as possible, and they're anxious to become acquainted with you. Never fall into the trap of thinking that your spirit teachers are too busy to help you. Remember: they "signed up" for this job. On the Other Side, your guides agreed to accept the commission of working with you from their place in the spirit world while you undertook another lifetime. We'll discuss this process more in the chapter entitled "Reincarnation and Other Lifetimes," but for now, keep in mind that your spirit teachers are excited to have the opportunity to learn and grow with you in their capacity as guides.

It's easiest for us to communicate with those in Spirit when our psychic receptors are open, and meditation is one method that opens these energy centers to receive input. There are many types of meditations, from guided visualizations to mantra chants to movement meditations, that help the spiritual student connect with the Divine and thus center and balance the soul, which is the true purpose of meditation.

When we are peaceful, quiet, and open to receive, Spirit can speak to us without interference. Meditation teaches us how to settle into the still point within, where Divinity resides, so that we can reconnect with this inherent part of ourselves. This beautiful and divine still point also connects us to every other sentient being on the earth plane and in the entire Universe. It is in this place that we shift our perception in a way that allows us to receive guidance, wisdom, information, and inspiration from our spirit guides, teachers, and angels. It also allows us to access our loved ones who have passed into Spirit. Eventually, a student develops to the point where, without having to do lengthy meditation work, she can make this perception shift to access the spirit realms within. Meditation, though, still remains an important component of the spiritual pathwork, because without inner peace, no peace can be achieved in life.

I've never meditated before. How do I get started?

Meditation is, first and foremost, a method of relaxing the body and quieting the mind. It does take practice, but it's something that anyone can learn. Take a moment now to breathe deeply as you continue reading. Breathing is an essential component of meditation, and most people do not breathe deeply in their everyday lives. A complete and deep breath should fill your abdomen, pushing down the dome-shaped muscle there called the diaphragm, which helps to expel breath during exhalation.

Right now, put your hand on the lower section of your abdomen, below your navel. Breathe in, and see if you can fill your belly enough to push your hand out as it rests there. If you can, then you are breathing correctly, which will help you in your meditation practice. If you have trouble with this, practice taking another deep breath in, which will cause the hand on your belly to rise. Exhale, and keep pushing all of the air out of your abdomen and lungs as your hand sinks back toward your spine. The more you practice this, the better you will become at deep breathing. Try counting as you breathe in and out, too: start by inhaling to a count of seven, hold the breath for a count of three, and then exhale to a count of fifteen. This may be a challenge for you, but the more you do it, the easier it will become. You will even get to the point where you can increase the counts on your breaths in and breaths out.

Why this emphasis on breathing? Breathing is what ties the mind to the body in meditation, and as you concentrate on your breath, other thoughts drift away. You may still have other thoughts, but you can silence them by bringing your attention back to your breath cycle any time they stray. Deep breathing also cleanses the energy centers of the body, the chakra and aura system, and relaxes the body so that the mind can open to spirit communication and the Divine Presence.

In the appendix of this book, there are two guided-meditation scripts to help you with different meditation experiences. Guided meditations can be read into a recording device and listened to on headphones to enhance your meditation practice. Many students new to mediumship development and spirit communication find guided meditations helpful as they're getting to know their spirit guides and making their first contacts with those on the Other Side. Eventually, if you practice your meditations on an everyday basis, you won't need to listen to guided meditations. You'll understand how to access the spirit world without them, and it will be a more natural process for you.

Is meditation the only way to make a connection with my spirit guide?

No. Meditation is the best way to connect with your spirit guides, especially if you want to work with them on a regular basis, but there are other ways to communicate with them. One of these is through dreamwork, during the sleep state. Many people have described encounters with their loved ones in their dreams, and we'll talk more about this phenomenon in the chapter "Messages from the Dearly Departed."

We can also access our spirit guides during dreams, but again this is a process that must be learned and practiced on a regular basis. Just as in meditation, many people try to connect with their guides and teachers through their dreams, and when it doesn't work the first time, they give up on the process. Did you give up the first time you encountered a difficult arithmetic problem in math class when you were a student? You might have felt like throwing in the towel when the problems got harder, but you knew that if you stuck with it and put forth some effort, you'd eventually understand the process and solve the problem. The same is true for dream-work with your guides. It's true for all communication processes with the spirit world.

In order to establish a link to Spirit in your dreams, you must first give your guides permission to work with you there, and you do this by stating this intention. Before you go to sleep, clear your mind and state, either aloud or in your thoughts, that you would like to meet with one of your spirit guides in your dreams. Hold this intention firmly in your mind and ask that this meeting be for your highest and best good. Expect that this will happen, and be prepared to record your experience by keeping a notebook and pen or a tape recorder next to your bed. You want to be able to write down or record any dreams that you have as soon as you wake up. Scribble down anything and everything you remember, or speak it into the tape recorder so that you can listen to it later. You need to do this immediately upon waking, because if you don't you will invariably forget your dreams, and thus your effort to meet your guide will be for naught.

If you don't recall anything when you wake up, it doesn't necessarily mean that you didn't meet your guide. Keep trying, and next time ask Spirit to help you remember the encounters that you have in your dreams. Keep in mind, too, that your spirit guides may appear in many mysterious or odd ways in your dreams. For example, you may recall nothing from your dream except for the color blue. Write this down, for you may find that your spirit guide wears a blue outfit and is using this color as a way for you to understand her nature or energy. You may see an animal in your dream. Perhaps this is one of your totem animals or a Native American guide. If you dream of something that doesn't seem related to spirit work, write it down anyway. You may find as you continue working that your spirit guide was in the dream somewhere and was trying to send you an important message through the use of symbolism.

Dreams are often filled with symbolism, and these symbols will usually be meaningful to your own mind in some way. If you ask for your spirit guide to work with you as you sleep and you dream of a waterfall, what significance might this have? Perhaps if you don't yet know anything about your guide, she's trying to tell you that her name is Falling Water. Or maybe the waterfall is symbolic of something that's happening in your life. What does water represent to you? Do you think of cleansing or bathing when you think of water? Is your guide trying to counsel you to wash something out of your life that is no longer needed? This is why keeping a journal to record your dreams is extremely helpful. You can write down your thoughts and feelings about the messages that come to you this way, which can be very beneficial in sorting out which particular spirit people are delivering these communications.

I talk to my guides aloud during the normal course of my day, and I believe this helps to facilitate my communication process with the spirit world. I speak to my guides about many things. Sometimes, I just like to say hello and tell them my thoughts on various feelings or tasks I have. Many times, I include them in my mental conversations as I'm making decisions or mapping out my schedule. If I need help with some mundane task, I ask for it, whether it's to get a close-in parking spot at the supermarket on a rainy day or to arrive at a meeting on time when a train blocks my normal route. And you don't have to know any of your guides intimately to ask for help with any of these things! Simply say, "Spirit guides, I know you're here with me. I need help with _____" (fill in the blank, and take as much time to state what you need as is necessary).

As I mentioned before, your guides want to work with you, but you must give them permission. By asking for their help, you're opening the door to some miraculous intervention, and you're also building a rapport that will enhance the spirit communication process. Don't be afraid to talk to them! If you feel silly doing it out loud, either wait until you're alone (your car is a good place for this), or simply think what you need to say in your mind. Spirit communication is mind to mind, and your guides will hear and understand your thoughts.

So, our guides hear and see us all the time? Even when we're . . . using the bathroom?

Your guides are not voyeurs. They're not interested in embarrassing you, and they understand the need for privacy when we're indisposed or spending intimate moments with a spouse or partner. And remember that your guides need your permission to work on your behalf. If you're ignoring your guides or aren't aware of their existence, they can check in on you to see how you're doing, but they can't interfere in your life. They do have a sense of when it's appropriate to check up on you and when it's not. So, no—they don't hang around in your bedroom while you're undressing. But if you call them when you're standing in your underwear, they will be there instantly. You have been warned.

How do I know if my spirit guide really hears me when I call him?

It's terribly difficult for us to trust something that we can't see, isn't it? We've been taught for so very long that the only real things in life are those we can see with our eyes, touch with our hands, or hear with our ears. Your spirit guides and teachers understand this doubt, because many of them had similar fears when they inhabited a physical body on the earth plane. The interesting thing that I've learned about spirit communication over the many years I've been practicing it is that the more you trust the connection between yourself and your guides, the stronger and more tangible it becomes.

Let's say you're new to spirit communication, and you've just realized you have a female guide with you. You think her name might be Iris because you've seen these flowers in your meditations, but you want to make sure. As you're driving to work one day, you say aloud in your car, "I would like to verify with my spirit guide that her name is Iris. If that's your name, please show me three irises by the end of the workday." There—you've given your spirit guide a very specific task, and you've built into it a way for her to verify a piece of information for you. It's now your job to pay attention for the rest of the workday to see if you get the verification for which you've asked.

So, you go into your office, and as you walk to your cubicle, you see that the floor secretary has a new bouquet of flowers on her desk. Among the blossoms is a lovely purple iris. There's one sign you asked for! You smile as you turn on your computer and put your coat away. When you sit down at your PC, you log onto the Internet, and as you're checking your favorite website, you spot an ad for a florist featuring a picture of beautiful blue irises. Two confirmations, right? But you asked for three, didn't you? A few more hours pass, and you go out to the local sandwich shop for lunch. As you're digging in your purse for your wallet to pay for your meal, you notice the song playing in the restaurant over the speakers: "Iris," by the Goo Goo Dolls. There are your three pieces of confirmation, and you can now be sure that your guide wishes to be called Iris when you communicate with her.

Do you see how this works? You asked your guide to verify something for you in a very specific way, and she was able to do it. It's not a coincidence, as many people might think. Could it merely be coincidence that you asked for verification of the name Iris, and you experienced three irises in the same day? I truly believe that there are no coincidences when dealing with the spirit world. And the more you trust that you will get an answer, the easier it is for Spirit to work with you and bring you the information you desire.

What other kinds of tasks can I ask my spirit guides to help me with?

Anything and everything! Your guides can help to manipulate energies around any given situation to bring success and happiness to you. The operative word here is *help*, however. You need to work toward your success and happiness as well. Your spirit guides aren't going to do it all for you. How would you learn your own spiritual lessons if that were the case?

For example, perhaps you need a new job. You can ask your spirit guides to help you find one that will be meaningful for you, that will satisfy your monetary needs, and that will be close to your home. Once you ask, though, you can't just sit around and wait for the job to drop into your lap! You must still act in accordance with the intention you've set—to acquire a new job—by updating your résumé, scheduling interviews, doing research within the job market, and so on. Your guides will be working behind the scenes, so to speak, moving energies, trying to remove obstacles and challenges from your path, and possibly bringing in more opportunities for you. Ultimately, it will be up to you to perform well in job interviews and to select which new position to accept, but your guides can help you make a good impression and to choose wisely in the decision-making process.

Trusting the information we receive is, without a doubt, the hardest thing about this work. All of us want to be correct in the things we say to others and in the decisions we make for ourselves. If you want to become a professional medium and contact Spirit to help others in readings or counseling sessions, you need to practice these skills for a long period of time so that your trust in your guides is implicit. You can't be second-guessing what Spirit brings to you when you're working with a client. In a more personal setting, Spirit understands our doubts, but we must work to overcome them in our communications with our guides and teachers. I don't believe the spirit people are ever wrong about the information that they bring to us. We may misinterpret the information that comes through, though, because the process itself is flawed. We may receive a piece of information through clairvoyance, or by seeing a picture or vision in our mind, but we may not completely understand what we see or how it pertains to the question at hand. We may hear a message in our inner, clairaudient ears, but we may only hear part of a sentence or a word. A vital piece of it may be missing, and so the process is not perfect. Through our clairsentience, we may feel strongly that we should or should not do something, but we may only get one feeling when Spirit may be trying to send us a more complicated message.

Thus, at times, the messages are incomplete, or we misinterpret them and then find out later what we were really meant to understand. Spirit communication is difficult at times, and why shouldn't it be? Communicating with people who are physically present in our lives is often complicated, too, and we often have misunderstandings with our family and friends, don't we? It makes sense that this would happen in the course of a spirit communication at times as well. Having said that, it's been my experience that the more you communicate with your spirit guides and teachers, the better the rapport you establish with them, and the easier it becomes for you all to understand how to communicate clearly with each other. Refining this process takes work and dedication, but it's worth it. You'll find yourself to be a much more focused, happy, and successful person once you're able to trust your guides and teachers, and realize the depth and breadth of their love for you.

I've been able to connect with one of my guides in meditation, but every time I meditate, he looks different to me. Why? How do I know it's the same guide?

Sometimes our spirit guides will appear in a different guise because it's part of a message they're trying to impart. For instance, perhaps your spirit teacher who normally appears bearded comes into a meditation one night clean-shaven. What could this mean? Perhaps he's been trying to help you with a particularly annoying problem, and this is his way of letting you know that this irritation (the beard) is now gone, and you're starting with a clean slate (the smooth skin). Or, typically dressed in green, your spirit guide appears in your next meditation wearing a yellow outfit. What could this mean? If you know the symbolic meanings of colors (which you'll need to study if you're a serious mediumship student), you'd recognize that your guide is telling you to expect more knowledge, wisdom, or learning in your life soon. Just by changing the color of her outfit, she may be encouraging you to study something or to read a certain book.

But how do you know this for sure? This is one of the challenges of spirit contact, and it's one that deters many students, because it takes a while to establish a consistent mode of communication. You may have to work long and hard with your guides to set up a kind of psychic shorthand between yourselves so that you can understand the meanings of their communications without a shadow of doubt. This usually entails a good understanding of universal symbolism and working diligently with your guides on when and how to use this symbolism to impart messages. Again, the more you work at this, the easier and clearer your communications with Spirit will become. No one ever said that mediumship was easy. Nothing worthwhile ever is.

So, how can you be sure that the same guide is getting in touch with you through your meditation work? This is where the most important rule of mediumship comes in. That rule is *you control Spirit*, and you must establish from the beginning of the communication process what you can and cannot tolerate with your guides. You need to instruct them in the best way to communicate with you, and then make adjustments to the process as you try new things and see how they work out.

For example, if you tell your spirit guide the first time you meet her that you need her to stand on your right side when you're working together, she'll always come in on your right side. You'll feel the energy on the right side of your body change when she comes through (using your psychic sense of clairsentience), or you'll see her in your meditation (using your psychic sense of clairvoyance) standing just to the right of you. If you're clairaudient (the psychic sense of hearing Spirit), you'll hear her voice in your right ear.

You've now taken control of the spirit contact, and you'll be certain that whenever you feel, see, or hear Spirit on your right side, it's that particular guide coming through. You won't have to guess which guide it is, because you've established this protocol with all of your guides. Your other guides may be assigned different places to stand around you, which will further help you to understand which guide is working with you when you're communicating with Spirit. This also allows you to recognize additional messages that may come in from certain guides. For instance, if your guide always stands on your right, and she always comes in with the color purple, you'll instantly know that she has a new message for you if you feel her come in on your right side but the color you see clairvoyantly over there is blue. You can then use your knowledge of symbolism to interpret the color she's brought to you and the meaning of the message.

I've been told by two different mediums two different names for my guide. How do I know which name is correct?

Well, how do you know for sure that the mediums who gave you those names were picking up the same guide when they identified him? Remember that you do have more than one guide working with you, and it's possible that the mediums you consulted were picking up different guide energies and thus gave you the names of two separate entities. If the mediums were actually receiving messages from the same guide, one or both of them could have misinterpreted the information that came through, or perhaps they only heard part of the name that Spirit was trying to impart.

If you've been given a name for a guide, you're the person who will be using that name, and you're the one who must be comfortable with it. For instance, when I first began studying mediumship, I was given the name *Dr. Jones* while sitting in a development class. Another student identified the guide that I know as my doctor teacher; I recognized the physical description of this spirit when he brought through the message. The medium, however, said that the guide was named Dr. Jones, and I'd been calling my doctor teacher Dr. Wilkins. Was the medium wrong, or was I?

I struggled with this for some time before I finally decided that it was more important that I be comfortable with the name I called my guide, and every time I tried to use the name Dr. Jones, all I could think of was Indiana Jones, the film hero I'd had a crush on for as long as I could remember. Humorous, yes (and humor isn't necessarily a bad thing when working with Spirit), but I decided I needed to be a little more serious when dealing with my guides. For this reason, I stuck with the name Dr. Wilkins, and I'm confident now that this is the name my guide recognizes when I call for him. If I started calling him Dr. Jones now, eventually he'd get the hang of it and would respond, but why mess up a good thing? He'll remain Dr. Wilkins to me for the rest of this incarnation. If, when I get to the Other Side, he tells me his name really is Dr. Jones, I figure we'll have a good laugh about the whole thing.

Many people get stuck on the issue of names while trying to learn more about their guides. In my work with Spirit over these many years, I've discovered that our spirit friends really don't care what we call them, as long as we feel comfortable with the name. Again, their goal is always to make the communication process as simple as possible. In fact, you don't even have to call them by any name at all. You can address them as "Hey, you" for the rest of your life, and they'll still be able to respond to your needs and petitions for assistance. Having a name, though, makes it easier to communicate with them, and since clear communication is the goal, the more you use a particular name, the more your guide will understand your needs and respond to them.

How can I discover the best name to call my guide?

Working with your guide in meditation is a great way to find out the name your guide favors and what suits you best when communicating with her. In your meditations, you can specifically set the intention that you wish to know the name of the guide with whom you're connecting. Then, it's vital that you pay attention to every detail of your meditation experience to figure out the name your guide is trying to bring to you.

Not every guide comes into a meditation and says, clear as day, "Hi, my name is Running Bear." Instead, you may receive a clairvoyant image of a big grizzly bear loping along the side of a mountain. You may hear part of the name, perhaps just the *buh* sound, or you may feel all warm and fuzzy and have no idea how this applies to a name.

When you're unclear about the message that your guide is trying to impart, you need to ask for more information, or tell your guide to give you the name in a different way. You can also ask for something to be shown to you in your waking life that will answer your question. For instance, let's say you only received the warm, fuzzy feeling in your meditation when you asked for your guide's name. When your meditation is finished, say to your guide, "Thank you for what you gave to me, but I still don't understand what your name is. Can you please show me a picture sometime tonight that makes sense as your name?"

Be sure to be specific about how you expect the message to be delivered: *show me a picture tonight.* Then, be extra careful to pay attention the entire evening to receive the message your guide will be sending. Maybe at some point, you're paging through the newspaper, and you see an advertisement for the local zoo. There's an image of a polar bear swimming underwater. As soon as you see it, you sense that warm, fuzzy feeling again, and you realize that your guide has a "bear" name. Now, your guide may prefer the name Running Bear, but at least he was able to help you understand the "bear" part of his name. Perhaps at another time, he'll be able to impart the "running" designation, too. But you received the message! Good for you both.

Do you see how sometimes messages are like piecing together a puzzle? This is what's both fascinating and frustrating about spirit communication. But believe me, the process gets easier as you practice it, and the benefits of knowing your guides and teachers far outweigh any aggravation that may arise from the imperfect process of mind-to-mind communication.

I call my guide, but he doesn't answer. Why?

Are you sure he's not answering? It's been my experience that guides always come when we have need of them, but we may not be aware of their presence because we're too wrapped up in the conflict or emotion of the moment. As you work more on developing a relationship with your guides, you'll become acutely aware of when your guides are present. And if they aren't present and you want them to be, you simply need to call them in, and they *will* be there.

If you want to be more perceptive about your guide's presence when you ask for him, try working on some awareness exercises for your physical self. The more honed our physical senses, the better we're able to receive and understand our nonphysical senses—those usually referred to as the "clairs." We've already discussed the most common ones.

To review: *clairvoyance* is the ability to see Spirit or to receive visual images when communicating with the other realms. *Clairaudience* is the ability to hear spirit voices or other sounds with your inner ear. *Clairsentience* is the ability to feel the presence of spirit entities or to use reactions in the physical body to perceive and interpret Spirit messages. *Claircognizance* is the ability to know instantly and without a doubt what Spirit is imparting—the message comes through in the mind as an assured knowing. *Clairgustance* is the ability to smell odors and taste flavors that Spirit sends to you. All of these perceptive abilities correspond to our physical senses of sight, hearing, touch, taste, and smell. By paying more attention to our physical senses and the information that we receive through them, we can also become more aware of our clairs and understand better when Spirit is sending us a message using these extra senses.

For instance, if you'd like to strengthen your clairvoyance, work on becoming more observant every day. If you go to a shopping mall, take fifteen minutes to sit on a bench and really watch the people as they go by. Pretend you're witnessing a crime and must give a report to a police officer. Notice everything—hair color and ornaments, clothing style, types of shoes, whether bags are slung over left or right shoulders.

Does the lady in the denim jacket have blue or brown eyes? What kind of glasses is the man in the red raincoat wearing? Does he have a moustache? Is it bushy or thin? Quiet visual observation helps us to realize the details of the world around us, and thus makes us more aware of subtle changes that may happen when Spirit moves in.

Now take this exercise a step further and ask your spirit guide to work with you to enhance your clairvoyance. Sit with your eyes open and stare at a fixed point on the wall ahead of you. If you wear spectacles or contact lenses, remove them, and stare at that fixed point with soft eyes. If your eyes wander, bring them back to the same point. You can blink, but keep your eyes on the spot you've chosen.

After a few moments, the edges of your vision will begin to soften and blur. Keep staring at the point on the wall. Eventually you may notice the areas at the corner of your vision begin to fill with mist or clouds, and you may see movement as well. Don't alter your line of vision in an attempt to see these more clearly; keep your eyes trained on that stationary point. Even though you're not looking directly at these clouds or the movement among them, you'll still be able to see what's taking shape there.

And what exactly are you observing? Nothing less than the inhabitants and the landscape of the Other Side! Remember that the spirit world surrounds us at all times, so it makes sense that you'd be able to visually observe it if you knew how. This exercise, called *transfixing* and developed by medium Sharon Anne Klingler, has enabled you to do just that. You may see the forms of people passing or standing nearby. You may notice the cut of a sleeve or the bottom of a robe or dress. Don't worry if you can't see faces, or if you can't determine the gender of those around you. Just being able to see these figures is an exciting achievement in your spirit work. If you continue to practice transfixing, you'll be able to shift your perception so that you can see more details of those in the spirit world more clearly. You'll then be able to use this sense to identify those that are with you, whether they're spirit guides, angels, or loved ones who have passed over. But in order for you to see them, you must practice. And once you can see them clearly and easily, you'll never doubt again that your guide is with you.

I asked my guide to help me find my lost yearbook, but so far I haven't had any luck. What gives?
It's great that you've recognized that you can and should ask your guides for aid with mundane matters. Requesting help in locating lost items is a good way for Spirit to work with you and for you to practice your communication skills. It will also reinforce for you, once you actually *find* the lost item, the reality of your guide's presence and his willingness to help you. Herein lies the challenge for many of us, so let's look at this dilemma with a fresh perspective.

It's fine and worthwhile to request that your guide help you find something. Saying aloud, "Hey, Daisy (or whatever your guide's name is), I can't find my yearbook. Can you help me?" lets Daisy know that you need her aid. It may be that you and Daisy have been working together for so long that she doesn't need anything more than that request, and later in the day you'll come across the yearbook while taking the trash out to the garage. If this happens, be sure to thank Daisy loudly and profusely for saving you from a long, arduous process. You may discover that you need to do some work along with Daisy, though, and using a logical, systematic approach might be the key. Asking for Daisy's intercession is always the first step, however, because she can't help you at all unless you ask.

Once you've asked (and thus set your intention to find the yearbook), spend some quiet moments reviewing in your mind the last time you saw your lost item. Granted, if it was ten years ago, this can make the task a bit more daunting, but nothing is impossible for Spirit! Perhaps you remember looking at the yearbook a few months back when you ran into an old classmate at the grocery store. Where were you sitting when you looked at it? If you can't remember, ask Daisy to help jog your memory.

Close your eyes and visualize the interior of your home. Go through each room and attempt to "see" yourself in that room, looking at the yearbook. Most likely, when you reach the room where you actually did read the yearbook, it will somehow stand out to you. It may seem brighter when you look at it, or it may radiate some sort of active energy. You may simply know, "That's it!" These are all legitimate ways to get an answer, and neither is better or worse than any other method. Once you know a room to start with, ask Daisy to highlight the area of the room where you should begin looking. Again, observe how this knowledge comes to you, and trust what you get. When you've got things narrowed down a bit, start looking for that book. Chances are, you'll find it.

What if you don't find it after receiving information from your guide? Perhaps you're misinterpreting the information. Are there other meanings that a picture you're seeing could have? I've found the room-by-room method to be one of the best for locating lost items, but it's something I've had to work on for a long time, and sometimes I haven't found what I'm looking for. What about other people who may live in the same house as you? Could your spouse or child have moved the yearbook after you'd left it in the place your guide has indicated? Ask about this, and see what kind of an answer you receive. Pay attention to the images or feelings that you get, and follow up on those to rule out any other possibilities.

More than likely, if you approach the problem step-by-step, working in tandem with Spirit, you'll find what's been misplaced. At times, though, you may not, and you may need to face the fact that the item could be truly gone—meaning that it's served its purpose in your life, and you won't be getting it back. You can certainly petition your guides and the angels (and even those special "lost item" saints like Saint Jude and Saint Anthony), but it may be that you're not meant to have your yearbook. Why not? I'm not sure I can answer that question, but I tend to look at things very symbolically after working with Spirit for so many years. Maybe you need to stop looking at your past and live in the moment, or you need to be planning for the future instead of dwelling on times that are gone. If you meditate on this question, I'm sure Spirit will help you discover an answer, even if Daisy can't bring that yearbook back to you.

What do spirit guides think about us if we don't know about them or don't communicate with them very often?

Spirit guides and teachers are the epitome of the word *love*. They love us unconditionally, no matter who we are or how we spend our time, because they're able to see us with compassionate eyes and understanding hearts. Most of them have also had a human experience at some point in this physical plane, and so they realize that many of us are so wrapped up in our "Earth experience" that we haven't learned to make time for a spiritual one.

Our guides and teachers agreed to assume these roles for us as we go through this lifetime, and they do this because they love us. They also know that they themselves will grow spiritually from the experience, whether they spend the entire lifetime working with us or standing around, twiddling their ethereal thumbs. No matter what choices we make in our lifetimes, our guides are here to support us and to exercise unconditional love.

Do they get frustrated with us if we ignore them? No, even though we often get frustrated with them, thinking that they just don't "get it" when we want something and assume they aren't pulling their weight to help us achieve it. Those in Spirit have a much broader vision and understanding, and they don't get stuck in the earthly concerns that often consume us. They know that we're all still learning, and that we're all in exactly the right place from a spiritual perspective. They pray for us and send us love, whether we know about them or not. And if we do know about them, they don't judge our actions, or us, for they know that everything we do, say, feel, or enact is between Creator and us.

You mentioned that our guides grow spiritually by helping us. If we don't know about them, how can they accomplish this?

Naturally, every spirit guide working with a human being wants to be known and valued. Very often, however, individuals having a physical experience are not introduced to the concept of spirit guides, and so their spirit teachers go along with them through their lives without ever being recognized or accepted. Spirit guides understand, however, that it may not be in the life plan of their particular protégé to develop an intimate relationship with their spirit people. This does not mean, however, that these "unknown" spirit guides have nothing to do for the eighty-odd years that their physical counterpart is alive. Spirit guides still have a rich and valuable life that they're leading in the other planes of existence, and we'll examine this further in the chapter entitled "The Other Side."

Even though our spirit guides are intrinsically connected to us, they're still free to do other things when they're not working directly with us, and they do exercise this freedom. They're still able, however, to keep an eye on us, and they know instantly if there's a need that we have that they may be able to fulfill. Probably the closest thing that those of us living a physical experience can liken this to is the intuition that a parent may have concerning a need for her child. We've all heard stories, or perhaps can remember a time as a parent, when a child has been in dire straits, and that protective, parental instinct has kicked in, notifying the mother or father to rush to the youngster's aid.

The energetic connection that we have to our spirit guides is similar in nature. If we're having a bad time, our guides and teachers are acutely aware of it, and they'll try to buoy our outlook or prospects so that we may feel better or more in control. They cannot interfere by changing the situation—they can only do this if we ask for their intercession, and even then it's mostly up to us to make the changes that are needed—but they certainly can pray for us, send us healing and positive energy, and generally surround us with invisible support. This might not sound like much, but these energies can be vital in helping us to progress and to learn our lessons as we encounter challenges in our lives. And as our guides send us energy, encourage us mentally, or project healing to us, they advance spiritually in their roles as teachers and guides.

Just how active can the role of a spirit guide be when we're not aware of him? I posed this question to my master guide, Merlin, whom I met at the age of eighteen but really didn't understand or believe in until my mid-twenties. As I held this question in my mind, a memory formed there, something I hadn't remembered for a very long time. I saw myself as a young girl, no more than seven or eight, at my grandparents' house on a bright summer day. My brother was there with me, but being older and a boy, he couldn't be bothered to play with his bored baby sister. I wandered from spot to spot in my grandparents' yard, wishing first that my mother would hurry up and finish whatever she was doing with my grandmother inside the house, then hoping that my brother would change his mind and introduce a game to me, then finally longing for a friend of my own—someone I could play with to pass the time until we could go home.

Dramatically, I wished this last and threw myself down on the grass, right next to a huge blue spruce tree that grew on the edge of my grandparents' property. A low branch, with its sticky needles, brushed against my bare leg, and when I looked at it, I noticed two eyes staring back into mine. I froze, frightened for a moment, until I realized the eyes belonged to a cat hidden in the thick shadows beneath the tree. Not being a cat person but hungry for any attention, I smiled and held out my palm, and, surprisingly, the cat bumped its whiskers against the side of my hand. It allowed me to run my fingers down along the slope of its back and to scratch its pert ears, and I enjoyed the rest of my time at my grandparents' house that afternoon with a black-and-white friend nestled in my lap. When it was time to leave, the cat darted back underneath the tree, and I don't remember ever seeing it again.

I smile now to recall this story, and to understand the message that Merlin is trying to impart by prompting its memory. I'd not known Merlin then, although I realize now that he has been with me in this incarnation since my first breath. But when I wished that day for a friend, it was Merlin who brought that cat to me to keep me company. The knowledge of this intercession brings tears to my eyes and a lump to my throat now. This is how much Spirit cares for us, whether we understand and acknowledge that love or not.

Is it better to communicate with my spirit guides or with my angels? Whose advice or guidance is better?

Like any other relationship you have in life, you'll find that certain connections with spirit entities are easier to nurture, understand, and maintain than others. This has everything to do with your own unique energy and nothing to do with labels such as "better" or "worse." All spirit guides and angels can work with you, lend you support, aid you in every way possible, bring you clear messages, and so on.

No one guide is better than another, just as no particular human being is better than another. All people have been created with an intrinsic divinity, which connects us back to our Creator and reminds us that we are all divine and should be honored and respected as such. Angels, while not human, carry their own spark of divinity and maintain their own connection to Creator while fulfilling their roles as helpers to humanity. You may find yourself attracted to working more with angels than with guides, or you may discover that the opposite is true. *Whatever feels best for you is the right way!* And it may be different for you than it is for your spouse, child, or best friend.

When I first began working with Spirit, I was taught about guides, and I found that I had a great affinity for guide energies. Within my own band of guides, I discovered that I worked best with Mara, my joy guide, and Merlin, my master guide. A few years after I'd begun working with my spirit guides, I started to become more and more interested in angels, and I began working with their energies as well. Two years ago, the Archangel Metatron came to me in a meditation, and I now work very closely with him. As you progress, you may grow and change, and the guides and angels with whom you work may also change. Your core group of spirit guides will always remain with you, but you may need different energies at various times in your life for particular reasons.

Your guides and angels understand that this is all a part of your unique spiritual development process, and they honor and respect that path. You'll never offend your spirit guide if you choose to work more closely with an angel for a period of time. You'll never upset one of your spirit guides if there's another teacher that's better suited to work with you on a certain project. Your guides and the angels are only interested in your highest and best progression, and they want you to have the best help possible. Jealousy and arrogance are feelings that spirit guides and angels have moved past in their own natures.

Why do I sometimes feel all tingly or shaky after praying to Jesus/God/ Creator, or after I meditate with my angels or guides?

One of the Natural Laws of the Universe is the Law of Vibration, which states that everything in the Universe vibrates. Science shows us that all matter is made up of molecules, and these molecules and their components are in constant motion. Even stationary objects, like the chair you're sitting in or the book you're holding in your hands, are vibrating, because the molecules within them are moving. The more dense and heavy an object or substance, the slower the molecules move, thus the slower the vibration. Those dwelling in the spirit realms— whether they're dead relatives, spirit guides, the Ascended

Master Jesus, or Creator—are pure energy, with no physical or structural body to make them heavier or more dense, meaning that their particular energies vibrate at higher speeds than ours.

The Natural Law of Vibration is the Law that governs mediumship because, in order for us to communicate with those in Spirit, we have to speed up our energy vibration. Spirit has to slow its energy vibration down, and then we are able to meet somewhere in the middle to make communication possible. Even though a spirit entity slows down her vibration to communicate with you, she's still vibrating at a much faster rate of speed than you are. You may notice this, then, when one of your spirit guides draws close to you during a meditation.

Let's say you ask for your doctor teacher guide to communicate with you in your meditation, and you suddenly feel a tingling sensation in your hands or feet. Tremors may run through you even though you're still controlling your breathing to maintain your meditative state. This is because your guide has come in close to you, as you asked him to do, and his higher-energy vibration is affecting yours. Prayer is a similar process to meditation, so if you pray to the Master Jesus, you've invoked his energy and entreated him to be near you. Does it surprise you, then, when he draws close to you, and his heightened energy vibration makes you shake?

I'll never forget doing a ritual in my home with my husband present in the circle, and I invoked the Archangel Michael, who came into the sacred space right behind where my husband was sitting. It was a small room, and I'd forgotten to warn my husband that he might feel the energies shift. Immediately after I'd invoked Michael, I noticed that all of the color had drained from my husband's face, and his breathing was shallow, as if he'd run a race. I asked him what was wrong, and he whispered, "I don't know what you did, but there's something really big standing right behind me." I assured him that it was Archangel Michael, nothing to be frightened of, and encouraged him to take some deep breaths. Needless to say, my husband had quite an experience that night with the Law of Vibration in action! If you experience something similar when you pray or meditate, ask Spirit to step back just a bit until you get more used to the higher vibrations that are affecting yours. After some time, you'll feel better and will no longer be adversely affected by the change in energy.

How can Jesus or the angels be helping 100 people in different places if we all ask for aid at the same time?

This question goes back to our discussion about energy and vibration. Angels, master guides (every person has a master guide), and Ascended Masters (like Jesus, Buddha, Saint Germain, and many others) all have very high spiritual vibrations. In the case of master guides and Ascended Masters, this reflects their work toward their own spiritual attainment and progression; with angels, it reflects their nature, the way they were created by the Divine. Because they've attained a very high spiritual energy, these entities are able to be in more than one place at a time (or many more places, if this is what's needed) and can communicate with more than one person at a time. We human beings have a hard time accepting or understanding this concept because we're unable to do this ourselves. I often joke that if I could just learn to bi-locate, I'd get a lot more done every day! But if ten thousand people are calling for aid from the Master Jesus at the same time, he can hear, understand, and send what is needed to each and every individual person that has asked for him, be-cause he has a higher spiritual nature than we do, and he's able to somehow manipulate energy in a way to make this happen.

I believe that someday perhaps our scientists here in the physical body may be able to replicate this process, at least in a limited way. Maybe they'll discover a way to enable a person to travel from one place to another by speeding up the par-ticles of energy until the body disappears, and then transport it to another place and slow the particles back down again so that the body reappears. It may sound very *Star Trek*, but I wouldn't be surprised if we can discover the means to do this . . . or, have it revealed to us by someone in Spirit that retains that knowledge and can communicate it to us. But the ability to be in many different places and understand the needs of many human souls—I think that's reserved for those entities that have progressed to a very high spiritual nature.

I think my grandmother is my spirit guide. Is this correct?

Traditional Spiritualist teachings tell us that a person has at least five spirit guides that come in with him when he's born and stay with him during his entire lifetime. He'll meet these guides again when his life ends and he returns to the Other Side. This means, then, that the people who share your physi-cal life with you as family members or friends cannot be your spirit guides, because they would not have been available in the spirit world since they were living their own incarnations.

Even if your grandmother passed away before you were born, it's unlikely that she was able to "become" a spirit guide, because there's more to this process than simply declaring your desire to be one (we'll discuss this in greater detail in the chapter "The Other Side"). However, spirit work is not an exact science. Sometimes, a beloved grandmother may pass away and decide from her new vantage point in the afterlife to play a major role in her grandson's life even though she's now in Spirit. Grandma can learn to communicate from the Other Side and send messages to her grandson, can influence his thoughts and feelings when making decisions, and can help to manipulate energies when needed, much like a spirit guide. For this reason, Grandma can take on an exceptionally important role from her place in the spirit world—but technically, no, she isn't your spirit guide. That doesn't mean, though, that she can't help you, and she can certainly still remain very close to you even though she's on the Other Side.

My circle of theatre friends has tightened over the many years we've known each other. We've all been through life challenges—marriages, divorces, children, illnesses—and yet I believe we know that, even though it was our love of theatre that brought us together, our love for each other as people cements the importance of these relationships and our dedication to maintaining them. I know that when I've needed a shoulder to lean on, my friends have been there to provide it. I don't feel alone, and I doubt I ever will.

Similarly, my team of spirit friends reminds me often that I have an invisible support system, too. As you must understand by now, getting to know your spirit guides, teachers, and angels can only enhance your life. The countless ways these friends can help you is only limited by your own imagination and willingness to connect with them. I hope you'll get to know yours better. It could be the best thing you ever do for yourself.

The Other Side

Imagine the most beautiful place you've ever been. Go on: close your eyes and recall a gorgeous landscape in the mountains, by the beach, in a lush forest, or anywhere else you've experienced an overwhelming sense of awe and wonder. Now sustain that feeling of amazing reverence . . . keep holding onto it . . . and you've got an ever-so-slight taste of what the afterlife is like. Add into that feeling a complete sense of peace, well-being, and ultimate acceptance for who and what you are, and you've moved a smidge closer to what you'll experience again once you reach the Other Side.

Marvelous, isn't it?

The truth is that no book can describe exactly what the afterlife is or everything that awaits us there. Some books, like *What Dreams May Come*, by Richard Matheson, depict the spirit planes through the eyes of someone experiencing them.

Interestingly, *What Dreams May Come* is a novel, a fictional tale of a man searching for his wife in the spirit world. Yet the list of references the author includes is an incredible collection of painstaking research done in order to bring as much validity to his story as possible. I highly recommend getting your own copy of this bibliography if you'd like to study more about the afterlife. Matheson himself says the following in his introduction to *What Dreams May Come*:

> Because its subject is survival after death, it is essential that you realize, before reading the story, that only one aspect of it is fictional: the characters and their relationships.
>
> *With few exceptions, every other detail is derived exclusively from research.* (Author's italics.)

Why would a novelist want so badly to get a story about the afterlife right? Any good fiction writer could have relied solely on his imagination and created any kind of setting and atmosphere he wanted to suit his tale. Although I cannot speak for Mr. Matheson, my sense is that he found his research about the afterlife so compelling that he wanted to convey it in the most accurate way possible. My wish is to do the same for you here by answering the questions people ask me so often about the Other Side. I've attempted to pull my answers from many different recorded sources about the afterlife (listed as references at the end of this book), along with what I've seen and experienced as a working medium.

Welcome to the world of Spirit. I sincerely hope you enjoy your tour.

What does the Other Side really look like?

Well, it isn't enveloped in clouds, but there are pearly gates.

In all seriousness, most sources indicate that the Other Side is very similar to our world here on Earth. Natural beauty abounds, including flowers and plant life, animals, and majestic mountains, plains, and bodies of water. Every type of environment is present in the planes of the afterlife, but all are moderate in temperature and comfortable for those who inhabit them. For instance, if someone really enjoys a desert setting, she can stay in the deserts of the afterlife for as long as she likes without worrying about heat exhaustion or dehydration. The temperature is pleasant and causes no discomfort to any of the beings dwelling there. More than likely, this refreshing and mild environment is one reason the afterlife has been dubbed "Summerland," to use an older Spiritualist term, bringing to mind cheerful memories of long, warm days and clear, temperate nights.

Along with natural settings, the Other Side also houses cities replete with magnificent structures. Any architectural delight found on Earth is also present in the afterlife, plus many more that we may not yet have here. There are buildings that become homes to transitioned souls as well as libraries, learning centers, concert halls, healing temples, and places of worship. There are bountiful green spaces, parks, and meditation gardens throughout the formal structures, providing places for souls to gather and commune. People on the Other Side can live in large group homes, like apartments or condominiums, or they can choose to live in private homes as close to or as far away from others as they like. The home becomes whatever the soul wants it to be. For instance, if a soul wants to live over a waterfall in a house made of red bricks, this will instantly manifest. Thoughts are things in the spirit world; all anyone need do is think a home into existence, and it will appear. Houses are not needed for protection—there is no body and thus no pain or physical death on the Other Side. Still, many souls love the experience of having a space of their own, and they like to continue it once they reach the spirit planes. And because space is infinite in the afterlife, just like time, there will never be a shortage of area where souls can dwell!

Although the Other Side resembles our physical world (or perhaps we should say that our world resembles the Other Side), there are some differences, too. Transportation is unnecessary in the afterlife, so there are no cars, trains, airplanes, or other mass transit systems. (This also means there is no pollution, or exploitation or destruction of the natural environment.) If someone wishes to travel, he merely needs to think of where he'd like to be, and instantly, he'll be there. There's no need for him to drive a car from point A to point B. However, some methods of transportation can be created by thought for the purposes of enjoyment. I've seen both bicycles and rowboats on the Other Side, but nothing that would run on gasoline or other fossil fuels. I've also been told that people can fly in the spirit world, if they can get past the impossibility of it in their own minds!

I did mention pearly gates, jokingly, but there is truth in that statement. The structures in the afterlife appear to our human eyes as almost too beautiful to describe. Shimmering light glances off the buildings as if they're made of luminescent pearls, glass, jewels, or precious metals like silver and gold. Again, these lovely places have been created through the collective, conscious thoughts of those who dwell there. Why not build them from the most breathtaking substances those minds can imagine? In the same way, the colors in the afterlife are much brighter and more vibrant than we can describe or experience here in the physical world. Dullness does not exist—everything resonates at the highest energy frequency possible, including the souls that live there. For this reason, the Other Side is absolutely resplendent with unmatched beauty.

What happens when we die?
What is the process of passing into Spirit like?

Over the last thirty years or so, many people have come forward to describe what are now called *near-death experiences*. Men and women from diverse cultures, backgrounds, ethnic groups, and age groups have recounted accidents, injuries, or illnesses that caused them to reach a state of clinical death. These narratives then continued on to describe processes by which their souls left their physical bodies, allowing them to experience the transition from this plane of existence to the next. If you read these accounts in books such as the groundbreaking *Life After Life*, by Raymond Moody, or *Hello From Heaven!*, by Bill and Judy Guggenheim, you notice patterns emerging in the narratives that make a strong case for the reality of an afterlife.

Most people who have had a near-death experience express a moment when they're able to see their physical body from another vantage point, often as if their consciousness is floating above the body. They recall a feeling of understanding that they're no longer in their body, and some recount a realization that they have died. At this point, different emotions may be felt or expressed, such as excitement, happiness, or, in more rare cases, apprehension or fear. If a negative emotion is experienced, it seems to only last for a moment or two, as the soul then begins to travel away from the body. This is often described as a rushing forward, usually accompanied by a feeling of warmth and love, and movement into a light that is bright and beautiful but in no way painful to look at or experience.

Having moved into this light, many souls next recall encountering an entity on the Other Side. Here, accounts vary somewhat. Some describe meeting with a passed loved one while others tell of speaking with a spirit introducing himself or herself as a guide or teacher. Some even recount a stirring experience with a great Ascended Master like Jesus Christ. No matter whom the soul meets, this seems to be when the person is told or shown by this entity that this is not the right time to enter into the world of Spirit, and the soul is either sent back to the physical plane, or is given the choice to come back, which the soul does. Almost every person who reports a near-death experience seems to re-enter the world of the living with a changed attitude. Many express a peace that they've never had before; quite often, they also talk about the fact that they no longer fear death. All seem forever changed by the experience in a very positive way.

By looking at these events, we can draw conclusions about what the transition from our physical life to the spirit world is like. We can also read transcripts from mediums and their sitters who contact departed souls now dwelling on the Other Side, who tell of their personal journeys to the afterlife. Accounts like these can be found in many books, including those written by celebrated mediums like John Edward, James Van Praagh, and Sylvia Browne. In these sessions, spirits often describe those who were waiting for them on the Other Side when they arrived and the great celebrations that took place, welcoming them home to the world of Spirit. We can rest assured that the transition process from this life to the next is filled with love, warmth, and joy. It is not something to dread or fear, because only beauty and love await us there.

My sister passed in an automobile accident. Was she in terrible pain when she died?

In my own sessions as a medium, I've had many spirits come through who have crossed to the Other Side as a result of accidents. Some have been in car wrecks; others have fallen from buildings, been trapped in fires, drowned, or died in industrial accidents. Many of these souls have taken these opportunities to reassure their loved ones that they felt no pain during their death. They've described a similar situation to the one recounted above, where the spirit is taken out of the body, and he or she may observe what is happening from another vantage point somewhere nearby. It seems to me that our spirit loved ones want us to know that they haven't suffered at the time of death, and that any guilt or fear about this issue that we carry should be released.

My mother passed after a debilitating illness. Is she better on the Other Side?

Every person who transitions to the Other Side goes through a similar process. When she arrives, she is greeted enthusiastically by loved ones who have passed before her and by her spirit guides and teachers that have worked with her during her incarnation. She then undergoes a process called a life review, where she witnesses all of her life experiences, reliving them and focusing on what she did or did not learn from these events. She judges for herself how well she accomplished the spiritual goals she made before her incarnation, and she reviews with her guides and teachers how she could have achieved more. This process takes as long as it needs to take for each individual—there is no time in Spirit and no timeline to meet. It happens in accordance with divine order.

Sometimes, if a person has been ill before her passing, or if she passes in a traumatic way, she may need time to heal from this upon arriving in the spirit world. In cases like these, the soul is taken by loved ones and guides to a healing institution, where the soul can rest, recuperate, and eventually assimilate again with the energy of the Other Side. The life review is put on hold until she is better able to remember who she is at a soul level as a divine being. This process takes as much time as necessary, but the vibration of the afterlife planes is very high, very loving, and incredibly healing.

Note that this healing is not physical, because there is no corporeal body any longer that is affected by cancer, diabetes, coronary problems, or any other maladies. The healing that is needed for many of these individuals is spiritual in nature; many physical ailments that afflict the body are results of poor mental, emotional, and spiritual states. Once the soul remembers the divine being that she is, she will exit the healing institution, take up her life review, and begin to enjoy the beauty and serenity of the Other Side. Any way it happens for her, her spirit will be renewed and whole.

My grandmother had dementia before she passed. I've heard that spirits retain their personalities after death. Does this mean she still has dementia?

Dementia is a mental disorder, like bipolar disorder, schizophrenia, or obsessive-compulsive disorder. Although these mental disorders may affect the personalities of living people, they do not carry over to the Other Side, where healing takes place completely. As mentioned above, some souls may need to undergo a special healing process that addresses their spiritual needs when they arrive in the afterlife, which brings about wholeness on every possible level.

Dementia was something that your grandmother chose in her life plan before incarnating so that she could learn a spiritual lesson from that experience. In her life review, she'll examine what she did or didn't learn from her mental illness, and she'll carry that knowledge forward as she continues to grow more in the afterlife. She will not, however, have dementia on the Other Side, and although she may make reference to it in a communication if she's ever given the chance to talk to someone from her place in Spirit, she won't display characteristics of that disorder any longer.

What kinds of things are people doing in the afterlife?

There are myriad activities and experiences awaiting all souls on the Other Side. As a mediumship teacher once told me, those in Spirit are not just sitting on a cloud playing a harp—unless this is something that a particular soul has chosen to do! We can spend our time doing anything we wish, as long as it's a positive, uplifting experience for us.

For example, I heard from one gentleman in Spirit who talked about fishing in the afterlife. His wife, the lady receiving the reading, grew puzzled and asked, "He's fishing in heaven? Really? He loved fishing here, but I didn't think he could do that in heaven!" Actually, yes, he *can* do that on the Other Side. Sports like fishing, golf, tennis, bowling . . . all of these are available to anyone who wishes to participate in them. It seems that all sports are played on the Other Side, with the exception of violent ones like boxing, wrestling, or those that rely on physical contact.

As a fan of hockey and football, I suppose I might miss seeing these sports as a spectator, but I know I won't regret their absence too much when I pass over—there will be too many other things to do. It's also important to realize that, in a sport like fishing, the fish are not harmed in any way. Once caught, they're returned to the waters, and they experience no trauma whatsoever. No matter what the sport, it seems there is no need for competition in the spirit world. People play for the exhilaration that they experience from the game, not because they want to beat somebody's score or be a champion. Feelings of competitiveness no longer apply.

The arts are very popular activities on the Other Side, too. Many souls decide to indulge in an artistic pursuit once they're in Spirit that perhaps they never had a chance to try in their physical lifetimes. Drawing, painting, and sculpting are activities that anyone can learn, allowing creative expression to flourish. This brings great joy to the soul, helping individuals to continue to evolve as spiritual beings, for all joy heightens energy vibration, moving us closer to the Divine. Positive performance arts like theatre also thrive. For those not inclined to create, there are many beautiful halls and buildings on the Other Side displaying wonderful pieces that can be appreciated by everyone in Spirit, thus elevating not only the vibration of each soul who chooses to witness them but also the collective energy of that particular plane of existence. Art has a very special place in the spirit world and is highly appreciated, and many enjoy performances presented by those who wish to entertain and inspire through artistic expression.

Music also plays an important role on the Other Side. Souls may choose to study music, learn to play instruments, or further their mastery of musical ability from physical lifetimes. Whatever the case, music permeates the planes of the Other Side because music also elevates the energy vibration of all beings. Souls often spend time at concerts given by musicians, enjoying the beautiful feelings that these performances evoke. All types of music that promote positive feelings are encouraged and created on the Other Side, lending to the overall beauty and serenity of the afterlife.

Probably the most important and popular pursuit in the afterlife is education. Because we're all spiritual beings, learning more about our progression to unite with our inner divinity is at the forefront of our experiences in the spirit world. This can take various forms, and many souls choose to attend classes or lectures—given by great masters and Ascended Masters, speakers, philosophers, and spiritual leaders—that focus on helping individuals to grow in their understanding of the Divine and their place in the Universe. Vast halls of learning reside in many locations on the Other Side, and often souls will spend a great deal of time in these institutions in order to enhance their knowledge by reading and experiencing lessons that others have recorded. Those that undertake these lessons are then able to apply the knowledge in classroom settings, meditation halls, and other experiential labs that allow them to see the wisdom of the masters in action. As they learn, these souls progress on their spiritual path, which is the goal of every spirit.

There is also work on the Other Side. For some of us, this may not sound appealing, but the work is only undertaken by those souls that wish to engage in it, offering another opportunity to many who long to continue their spiritual progression. Some souls may choose to become healers or counselors in the afterlife, where their job duties include helping those who have just made their transition to the spirit world acclimate to their new (and sometimes surprising) surroundings. My mother, who passed away in 2000, communicated to me on several occasions that, in the afterlife, she holds and rocks the babies that pass into Spirit as infants. Anyone who knew my mother can see how fitting this job is for her. Others may work to care for and play with the animals that transition to the afterlife. These beloved pets may have a long time to wait until their human counterparts arrive, and they need attention and love just as they did in the physical world.

Some people may wish to teach art, music, or other pursuits to interested souls or continue in the creative arts as artists, musicians, or performers. There are also those souls that go into scientific fields on the Other Side, perhaps just as they did in the physical world. There are great thinkers and intellectuals in the afterlife still making amazing discoveries and breakthroughs in the areas of physics and medicine. Many metaphysicians believe that these discoveries are then transferred from the spirit world to the minds of living doctors and scientists so that they may help those that are in the physical planes to live better lives. All of these jobs, and more, await those who pass into Spirit, and they're available for any who wish to fill them.

It's important to note, however, that the afterlife is not an experience of drudgery or obligation. All of the activities we've discussed are completely and totally voluntary and are available to all souls with the loving intention of helping them to expand their spiritual knowledge and advance their divine progression. They are, however, choices, and each individual may choose to pursue them, or he may choose to simply relax and rejuvenate on the Other Side. If a soul does work in any capacity, there's still plenty of time for that individual to enjoy the splendor and renewal that comes from life in Spirit. I've communicated with folks in the afterlife who describe their experiences of sitting by beautiful lakes, strolling through exquisite gardens, or attending uplifting and gorgeous concerts. Others that have spoken to me in readings have discussed even more "ordinary" activities, such as dancing with their spouses or children, playing cards with family members, or simply gathering and talking with beloved friends who had passed before them.

With so much to do and learn in the afterlife, it's amazing that souls there find time to communicate with those of us in the physical body, and yet they do. We'll discuss that in more detail in the chapter entitled "Messages from the Dearly Departed."

You talk a lot about choices in the afterlife.
Do you choose the "heaven" yourself, or is it predetermined for you?

There are many planes of existence in the afterlife. When we shed the physical body, our spirit goes to the plane best suited for us at our particular stage of spiritual evolvement. The Master Jesus describes this metaphorically in the gospel of John, chapter 14, verse 2, when he says, "In my Father's house are many mansions, and I am going to prepare a place for you."

Most major religions believe in an afterlife made up of levels that are attained based upon the goodness of the life lived by the individual transitioning to the Other Side. For instance, both Muslims and Christians believe in a day of judgment when God will separate souls and send one group to heaven (called Paradise by Muslims) and the other to hell. Christian doctrine delineates only between the much more pleasant realm of heaven for righteous souls and the miserable and fiery hell of souls found lacking because of their sinful natures. Muslims believe that Paradise is made up of seven levels, each more beautiful and luxurious than the last, where the resurrection of the physical body allows for physical pleasures. They, too, believe in a tortuous hell for nonbelievers and those who chose depraved actions.

In Tibetan Buddhism, the spirit goes through three stages, or *bardos*, after death; at the conclusion of the final bardo, the soul either enters nirvana or liberation from desire (which is believed to be the ultimate goal), or the soul returns to the physical plane through reincarnation (which we'll examine in more detail later). In Hinduism, souls may go to myriad heavens or hells for a period of time before entering into another physical rebirth, but all are believed to be illusory. The purpose of these, in Hindu belief, is to teach the spirit an attitude of detachment so that it may eventually achieve *moksha*, or liberation from the chain of death and rebirth. Jewish mysticism also reveals a belief in multiple heavens, implied in the Hebrew word *shamayim*, and there are thought to be seven heavens through which a soul may ascend.

The overwhelming prevalence of belief in multiple afterlife planes is, I think, a reflection of the reality on the Other Side. Although we cannot say for sure how many planes there are in the afterlife, we know there is more than one, and each plane has characteristics similar to Earth. Reports given by crossed-over spirits through mediumship communications reveal that souls are happy on the Other Side in the place where they arrive, but that each individual soul may work hard and move up into a higher plane upon achieving a new level in their soul progression. It appears that your level of spiritual evolution—which reflects the life you've lived, your actions and thoughts, and your application of the spiritual principles that all souls understand deep within—determines the plane of the afterlife where you end up.

Is there a resting period after death before a spirit can come through and communicate?

This does seem to be the case, although the actual period of time varies greatly from soul to soul. I've spoken to individuals that have been on the Other Side for decades, and to at least one that had only been there two days. If people ask me for a time frame, I usually recommend waiting at least six months after a loved one passes before consulting a medium to see if the loved one may come through.

It's important to remember, however, that there is no time in the spirit world as there is here in the physical plane. There is no sense of rushing to be on time for a meeting or of worrying about completing a project by a certain deadline. Each soul goes through his transition and acclimation to the afterlife at his own pace; there is no timeline for when he'll be ready, if ever, to communicate with those not in Spirit with him. Whether the soul is actually resting during this time is up to him as well. As mentioned before, some individuals need a healing period when they reach the Other Side. These folks may require extra aid adjusting to life in Spirit, and there will be healers, counselors, and guides to help them through this process. This has nothing to do with physical healing, as the soul is only energy in the spirit planes, but he may need help mentally and spiritually as he acclimates to his new existence. This may explain why it takes some souls a long time, by our measure, to communicate from the Other Side. There are other reasons communication may be hampered, however, and we'll examine that process later, in the chapter "Messages from the Dearly Departed."

Do pets go to the Other Side when they pass? If so, what do they do over there? Will we see them again?

As mentioned before, beloved pets do cross over to the Other Side, and they seem to have special places reserved for them on the planes of existence where their human counterparts will eventually end up. There are souls that have chosen to spend some of their time in the spirit realms looking after these animals and keeping them company until their people arrive. I've seen glimpses of wide-open areas of green fields and azure skies where dogs run and play with each other and these special caretakers. Cats, rabbits, hamsters, guinea pigs, goldfish, ferrets, horses—I've encountered all of these on the Other Side during readings with clients.

During a service at my church where spirit messages were delivered by different mediums, one message bearer brought through for a congregation member a chicken that she'd kept as a companion! This lady was ecstatic to hear that her dear chicken was safe on the Other Side. I'm sure there are other types of animals over there, too, if they were loved and nurtured by a human being. Anyone in Spirit can visit these animals, too, especially if they long for a pet or miss one from their physical lifetime. Children seem to be very drawn to playing with and caring for them. Pets are close friends to many of us, and they do wait patiently for us in the afterlife.

Do children and babies that pass into Spirit remain children on the Other Side?

It seems they do remain at the age of their passing for at least a while. This may be until they realize that, in the spirit planes, they can be any age they wish and assume any appearance they choose. Some souls may choose a path that allows them to "grow up" as they would in a physical body, bypassing the discomfort of different emotional stages or corporeal aches and pains, since these don't occur in the afterlife. Some souls may choose instead to assume an energetic form more in tune with the approximate "age" of their spirit once they've acclimated again to life in Spirit.

Souls that have been through the death and birth cycle many times often do not have as much adjusting to do once they reach the Other Side. Still others that pass as children may like themselves this way, and so they retain this "appearance." Many joy guides appear to be children; my guide Mara, no exception, looks to be between thirteen and fifteen years of age. The important thing to remember about the Other Side's children is that just because they assume the appearance of a child does not mean that their soul is inferior in some way. Many children in the afterlife are highly evolved entities and have progressed far in their spiritual journeys.

So, aging on the Other Side is a choice?

Yes. Remember that everything is energy in the afterlife, and thought vibrations can manipulate energy. The appearance of everything in Spirit is a combination of the thought vibrations of individuals and the collective consciousness of those sharing an experience there. For instance, let's say that two souls, friends during their last lifetime on Earth, wish to see each other in the afterlife. As long as they are both in a similar place in their spiritual evolvement, they need only send out the thought that they wish to find the other person, and instantly they will. Perhaps these friends decide that they'd like to have coffee together while sitting on a veranda, and without a moment's hesitation they will be transported to a scenic porch where a table and chairs, resplendent with their favorite beverages and all of the trimmings, await them. Although food and drink is not necessary to sustain the body on the Other Side, many folks still enjoy partaking of it, especially in a social setting, and they can have whatever they want simply by thinking of it.

The same is true of the appearance of each soul. If a spirit wishes to appear as a child, he will—with whatever hair, eye, or skin color he prefers, wearing whatever clothes he chooses. Many souls choose to retain the physical appearance of their last incarnation on Earth because they still feel close to this energy. Some, however, may wish to be younger or older than at the time of transition to Spirit, and this is perfectly acceptable. I have encountered many spirits in readings for clients that come through looking like a younger version of themselves, especially if they passed at an advanced age. It really has nothing to do with vanity—the soul chooses an appearance that makes him feel good, happy, confident, and loved, the energy that permeates everything on the Other Side.

My parents are both deceased. Are they together on the Other Side?

Once again, this is a choice made by the souls involved about how they wish to spend their time in the afterlife. Many of us incarnate in soul groups on the physical plane, and because the other souls in our group are very dear to us, we choose to see them regularly when we all transition to the spirit planes. Husbands and wives are often members of the same soul group, so it makes sense that they would spend time together once they return to Spirit. In the afterlife, however, we go beyond our human roles as husbands, wives, partners, family members, and so on. We once again recognize each other as divine beings with divine attributes, and we're not possessive or jealous of the relationships that our soul friends have with other souls. Therefore, we're not married on the Other Side, just as we're not someone's sister, cousin, brother, father, etc. When spirits come through in mediumship readings, they still identify themselves this way because they want the person with whom they're communicating to understand that the ties of love they have to each other are still intact. The love, however, transcends boundaries and definitions.

I've had husbands and wives come through in readings who describe seeing their spouses but not spending all of their time in that person's company. This simply means that these souls are continuing on in their spiritual development, and progression may not revolve around their relationship with the soul who was their spouse. When you think about it, it's really beautiful that we can all continue on in our spiritual journey, knowing that these other souls love and support us, no matter what our choices are. I've also had many spirits tell me in readings that they spend a great deal of time doing fun things with their spouse in the afterlife. I've even had divorced spouses come through to talk about reconciliation and the peace they've made with their broken families while in the spirit world, which is a great healing process for all involved. Again, all of these scenarios reflect the choices made by those participating in the relationships, and there are no right or wrong ways to pass time in the afterlife. It's essentially about the individual's soul progression and how others may or may not fit into it.

My best friend had a drug problem when he was alive. Will he be punished for it in the afterlife?

It's always difficult to see someone we love trapped in an addiction, whether it's drugs, alcohol, food, sex, shopping, gambling, gaming, or anything else that consumes a life. Understand, however, that your friend wrote this addiction into his life plan before he came into his physical incarnation, and he freely chose to undertake it. The purpose of any obstacle like an addiction is to challenge the individual on many different levels and, in doing so, to help him learn valuable lessons about his divine identity.

Some people will struggle and eventually overcome their addictions; some people may still have them when they pass away; some may even succumb to death because of them. No matter the circumstances, an addicted individual is loved just as much by Creator as any other person, and in Spirit his addiction will no longer rule him. It will be included in his life review, and he will see all of the things he did in order to feed his addiction. This is usually not a pleasant process for the individual reviewing his life, for he often acutely understands at this point the pain and suffering he caused others while in the throes of his addiction. Still, this should not be seen as a punishment. It's simply another lesson for him to comprehend as an evolving soul. How long it takes him to process this pain and heal from it is completely up to him.

What happens to murderers/rapists/bad guys on the Other Side? Where do they go? They are punished, right?

This is a difficult question to answer, because it may not be the answer you want or expect. There is no plane of the afterlife that is reserved exclusively for wrongdoers, which would be a similar concept to the hell of Christianity or Islam, where souls are punished for all eternity. Free will is an important component of our experience as spiritual beings, and yes, some people make horrible choices in exercising their free will. Most of us agree that murderers, rapists, terrorists, and the like deserve retribution for their crimes, and if these are not meted out during life (and perhaps even if they are), shouldn't the perpetrators be punished after death? What we fail to realize in this thirst for justice is that it does not serve our spiritual progression to insist on vengeance or vindication, even if we ourselves are victims of a crime.

I can relate to this myself. As a child, a family member molested me, and it took me a long time to deal with the emotional repercussions of that. I think I may still be dealing with them. It would be very easy for me to fall into a pattern of bitter, resentful, angry behavior stemming from this abuse. I realize, however, after many years of therapy, prayer, meditation, and reflection that this is a spiritual lesson in forgiveness that I need to learn. When I can look at this situation with more loving, objective eyes, I feel I move forward as a divine being. Whether I want to admit it or not, the man who molested me is also a divine being. Perhaps he was mentally ill and needed help to control his sick impulses; perhaps he was abused himself and was carrying out some type of twisted energy cycle.

These thoughts do not in any way justify what he did or make it any easier to accept, but they were challenges that this soul wrote into his own life plan before incarnating. And for whatever reason, I wrote the situation into my life plan, too. I try to remember this when I re-live a painful memory or have nightmares about the abuse. It's not easy, but dwelling on revenge or wallowing in a sense of self-pity or shame doesn't help me. It lowers my energy vibration instead of heightening it, which in turn attracts more negative things into my life. Who needs that? If you, like me, have been the victim of a crime, seek professional help and spiritual counseling so that you can deal with the past, heal from it, and move forward. Don't allow someone else's wrong choices to hold you back in your own life.

As mentioned earlier, we go to the plane of the afterlife for which we're best suited when we make our transition.

For troubled and criminal souls, there are levels replete with spirit counselors, therapists, and special guides and teachers that help them understand the huge, painful mistakes they've made. These souls undergo a life review just like every other soul, but their crimes are highlighted so that they can truly realize the incredibly negative impact they had on others. They spend a great deal of time focusing on their problems and working with the spirit counselors so they can begin to progress past the lack of compassion, empathy, and love they have for their fellow souls. They also work very hard on their own self-esteem and their feelings of self-hatred, which are often at the core of their issues. They go through very intensive spiritual rehabilitation, because Creator cares about these souls and wants them to succeed.

My niece committed suicide. What happens to her soul on the Other Side? Is she punished for taking her own life?

Suicide is an incredibly hard experience for everyone touched by it. The decision to take one's own life is usually prompted by intense and overwhelming feelings of doubt, fear, pain, anger, frustration, and hopelessness, just to name a few. Those left in the physical world when a loved one causes her own transition must deal with similar emotions like grief, anger, and shock. On top of all this, they often fear that their loved one will end up in a terrible place on the Other Side, possibly because their religion teaches them that there is no forgiveness from God for suicides, and she will be made to suffer in the afterlife. This is simply not the case.

When a suicide reaches the Other Side, she is met by her guides and loved ones, but she is also surrounded by special counselors who are experts in communicating with disturbed souls. These counselors accompany the soul as she reviews her life and try to aid her in spotting the troubling signs of distress that led up to her decision to take her own life. Together, the soul and the counselors examine her life plan and discuss what other choices could have been made to make things more bearable or to better execute the life lessons she'd laid out before her incarnation. It's important to note that suicide is *never* written into a soul's life plan. The negative repercussions of suicide are too great to the individual soul who chooses it, as well as to all the other souls whose lives are touched by the decision. Although this may not sound as negative as burning in a pit of fire for all eternity, the emotional and spiritual work that a soul must undertake after committing suicide is staggering and intense. It can continue for a very long time, but it is all a part of the soul's healing process and growth experience on the Other Side.

Well, some of this doesn't really sound fair. Although I believe God is loving and forgiving, it seems cruel that a suicide is happy and content on the Other Side while those left living struggle so hard with what she did. It seems wrong that a killer is rehabilitated instead of disciplined. Can you explain this?

I certainly can't pretend to know the Mind of Creator, but my sense is that struggling with our feelings about these challenging events and people are part of the never-ending learning cycle that we've undertaken as spiritual beings in a physical body. Perhaps they represent lessons in forgiveness. Maybe they teach us something about compassion and understanding. They may be ways to propel us to overcome our own hidden fears and live the life we've imagined. It's difficult to say what lessons these kinds of situations may highlight, but I believe that growing and learning occur as a result of every event we encounter if we can look at them with spiritual eyes. Some are easier and happier than others. Some are awesome in their scope, depth, and challenge. But each one brings us closer to realizing our potential and our perfection as divine beings.

I've heard about spirits that don't cross over to the Other Side. Why would this happen?

We discussed earlier the difference between a ghost and a spirit. A ghost chooses to remain in between the realm of the living and that of Spirit. Why would someone choose not to move on? Sometimes a soul may be held back by his memories. Unlike other spirits that experience intense euphoria after their transition, he may instead feel sadness in the face of leaving his earthly body and companions. He may long to complete a task he didn't have a chance to finish. He may feel compelled to remain with someone who mourns deeply for him and try to placate that sorrow by staying nearby.

Eventually, though, most souls realize that they're hindering themselves by not completing their transition to the Other Side. The light and energy of the afterlife continuously beckons to all souls that are in between the worlds, and the pull to go into that light and that energy will someday be too great for the lingering soul to resist. Again, there is no timeline for this to happen. It all hinges on the individual's choices and realizations, which only that individual can control.

I remember a woman who asked me if her sorrow for her deceased husband was holding him close to her and preventing him from completing his transition to the Other Side. He seemed to be an especially active spirit, constantly flipping the lights in their home on and off, playing with the television channels, and moving objects and pictures on the walls. I didn't feel, however, that she was holding him back in any way. He had completed his transition but was still able to affect energy in a very obvious way from his place on the Other Side.

Grief is a natural process that we all have to work through when we lose someone we love. It's wrong for us to blame ourselves for holding a spirit back, because that individual always has the power to choose to move on. We must remember, however, that it's unfair to ourselves to believe that our life cannot progress forward because we've lost someone special. It may take months or years to truly feel better after the loss of a friend, mate, child, or relative. Coming to terms with death often means facing our fears about this natural transition and sometimes tests deep, spiritual beliefs that we've held. But those whom we've lost always choose their own path, no matter what ours may hold. Seek help from a professional therapist, counselor, doctor, or minister if you have trouble letting go of your loved ones, but know that there is bountiful beauty and love awaiting them in the afterlife.

My father never believed in an afterlife. He thought that when you died, that was the end. What will he experience on the Other Side?

It seems that every soul, no matter what his personal beliefs, will experience the reality of the Other Side. I believe how quickly and easily this happens hinges on a soul's openness to new ideas and how quickly he remembers the spiritual planes from before his incarnation. In readings, I've had many spirits tell me they held very different ideas concerning the afterlife before they crossed over—but believe me, I haven't heard any complaints about what they've seen or done!

I had an interesting experience while doing a reading for a woman a few years ago. The session went very well, but toward the end of our time, she said, "I was really hoping to hear from my father." I always explain to my clients that no medium can guarantee which spirits will come through to communicate in a reading. If someone asks for a specific person, however, I'll try sending out my main message guide, Mara, to see if she can locate that loved one on the Other Side. When she comes back to me, Mara needs to deliver a very tangible piece of evidence that the sitter can quickly identify as pertinent to her loved one so that we know we've got the right soul. I asked for the name of the client's father and told her I would send out my guide to see if she could find him.

Moments later, a clairvoyant image began to form in my mind. I saw a man lying on the ground with his arms crossed over his chest, and he seemed to be in some sort of transparent bubble. There was another man standing close to him, and this man wore white robes, the type favored by some spirit teachers. This picture puzzled me, but I'd always been taught to give whatever I received in a session, because even if I don't understand it, the client might. I took a deep breath and said to my client, "I don't really know what this is, so I'm going to describe to you what I'm seeing." I proceeded to tell her exactly what was in my mind's eye, and when I began describing the physical characteristics of the man lying on the ground, the woman clapped her hands, delighted, and exclaimed, "That's my dad! He looked exactly like that!"

I was pleased to hear we'd indeed found her father, but this posed a problem for me: I couldn't communicate with him. He was completely unresponsive. His eyes were closed and he appeared to be asleep, no matter how loudly I called to him in my mind or how much Mara danced around him to capture his attention. Finally, I pushed a thought at the spirit guide standing near him. "Hey, are you his guide? What's going on with him?" His guide answered me very promptly: "He refuses to get up. He thought this world didn't exist, so he thinks if he keeps his eyes closed, we'll all eventually give up and go away. Little does he know, I've been putting up with his stubbornness for years, and I'm not going anywhere!" His guide went on to explain to me that he was working with the man, trying to make him aware of his surroundings so that he could begin acclimating and enjoying the Other Side, but so far he hadn't had much luck. "Well," the guide said cheerfully to me, "I've got all of eternity to get through to him!"

I related all of this to my client. When she heard what her dad was doing, she burst out laughing. "Yeah, that sounds like him," she agreed. "He always was more stubborn than a mule."

What I found out later was that this exact scenario is documented in a book called *Letters from the Afterlife: A Guide to the Other Side*, first published in 1914 by a woman named Elsa Barker. Ms. Barker received communications from a spirit named David Patterson Hatch, who was a judge when he lived on the earth plane. Judge Hatch began communicating with Ms. Barker through a process called automatic writing soon after his transition to the Other Side, and these communications are preserved in this book. At one point, Judge Hatch describes seeing a man lying in what appears to be a deep sleep in the afterlife, and Hatch's teacher awakens the man to help Hatch better understand the workings of free will, karma, and some other important spiritual lessons. How surprised I was to find verification of this phenomenon after Spirit showed it to me in a reading!

Peace. Beauty. Unconditional love. Learning and growth. All of these await our loved ones, and us, when we finish our lives here on the physical plane and cross over to the world of Spirit. You would think with this extraordinary atmosphere and the incredible opportunities presented there, our loved ones would forget all about their earthly existences. Spirit people, however, stay connected to those of us still retaining a physical body. The bonds of love are too strong to be forgotten. Read on in the next chapter to see how your loved ones may be trying to connect with you.

MESSAGES FROM THE DEARLY DEPARTED

Think about this: if you were dead, and you were only allowed to send one message to one beloved individual who remained in the living, what would you say? What message would be the most important to you to impart?

I'm OK!
I made it, and I'm well again!
Everything is fine here!
Or maybe, *I still love you!*

These are the messages I hear more than any others from people who have passed over to the Other Side. Assurances of happiness, peace, and well-being come through loud and clear from those that have made their transition. And even if it goes unspoken, the underlying message is always the same: *I will always love you. I will never forget you. I will never leave you alone.*

As a medium, I'm given the great privilege of meeting and working with hundreds of people every year, both in this physical world and in the spirit planes. I consider it an honor and a blessing to be able to reunite souls that have passed with the people still living who miss them so much. It is my job to try to bring their ethereal presences into sharp and absolute focus for the few moments they can spend with their loved ones in a reading setting, to, as one of my teachers, Reverend Janet Nohavec, calls it, "paint them back to life." This requires me to communicate with Spirit in a very special way, and we'll discuss this process more in the chapter entitled "Who, Me? A Medium?" But our spirit loved ones are constantly trying to remind us of their continued presence in our lives and of the great truth that life never ends. It just continues on in a different way.

In this chapter, we'll explore some of the ways your deceased loved ones may be trying to communicate every day. The more knowledge you have about this process, the easier it will become for you to be more aware of these communications and to believe in the reality of life after death. Our two worlds are very close; our loved ones are right beside us, whispering in our ears, spinning energies like webs around us, trying to get our attention. Let's stop ignoring them, and open our minds and hearts to understand their messages and meanings!

Why do I need a medium to communicate with my deceased loved ones? Can't I just do it myself?

Of course you can! That's really what this chapter of the book is all about. Everyone can communicate with relatives and friends on the Other Side, but many people just don't realize this possibility. If they do believe in the validity of communication, they may simply not understand how to make their connections stronger and more tangible. Keep reading for more information on how these ties to the Other Side can be strengthened and utilized.

As for mediums—we're *all* mediums. We all have the natural ability to discern messages from Spirit. Some of us are better at it than others, but everyone can learn enough to make their own connections to the spirit world meaningful. Consulting a professional medium is a wonderful idea, though, if you're having trouble making your connection and seek Spirit's counsel and assurances of love.

How can people who are supposed to be in heaven talk to us?

Our loved ones in Spirit can communicate with us in lots of different ways. Just like our spirit guides, teachers, and angels, they can use mind-to-mind communication—impressing images, thoughts, words, or songs in our brains as reminders of them or as symbols of what they want us to know. They can do this at random times—when we're washing the dishes or running the vacuum—or they can do it when we're actually concentrating on connecting with them, as in meditation. Either way, our minds link with theirs, and we're reminded of their presence and their love.

Once they have an understanding of the way energy works from the Other Side, our loved ones can manipulate it in various ways to send us messages. It's easy for them to use electronic devices, so they might make the telephone ring, turn appliances on or off, or cause the lights to flicker or blink. They might even direct the energy in such a way as to have a certain special song playing on your favorite station when you switch the radio on in your car. Many people ignore this or dismiss it as a coincidence, but please consider that your loved ones are working hard to move that energy, and they want you to know they're doing it for you!

Our loved ones may also communicate with us via signs. Perhaps your father was a birdwatcher when he was alive, and since his passing you've seen several red cardinals in your yard, even though it's the middle of winter. Whenever you see these birds, your mind turns immediately to your dad. Co-incidence? No! This is your father's special way of reminding you that he lives on in the world of Spirit, and he wants you to know that he's doing well and sending loving thoughts to you. These signs can be very simple or quite elaborate, as this next example shows. A client shared the following story with me, and it's proof positive that our loved ones really want us to know that they're still around us!

"My mother loved to shop, and while she was alive she drove a Buick LeSabre for years. About six months after she passed away, I was at a local mall, and a Buick LeSabre pulled out in front of me. I couldn't help noticing the license plate and was stunned to see the letters CBW and the number 4. My mother's initials are CBW, and she had four daughters. I knew it was a message from Mom! Even more surprising was that, a week later, my sister was at another mall in another part of town—and the same car, with the same license plate, pulled out right in front of her! We know this wasn't just a coincidence, and that Mom was letting us both know that she's still shopping with us."

Another way our loved ones can communicate from Spirit is through our dreams. When we sleep, the energy centers in our bodies open more fully, allowing us to access other states of consciousness more easily. Because most spirit communication happens in the mind, our loved ones are able to link with us as our minds drift through our sleep and dream states. Not every dream, however, is a visitation from Spirit. Dreams of loved ones that are incredibly vivid, sharp, and tangible, especially if you remember them well after you awaken, are more likely to be actual visitations from your spirit family and friends.

For example, perhaps you dream that you're sitting on a park bench next to your grandmother. The sky in the dream is a brilliant, blazing blue, and the nearby lake is calm and crystal clear in the sun. Your hair blows softly in the breeze, and you hear it stir the wind chimes in the tree across from you. Your grandmother smiles and takes your hand, and you feel the pressure of her fingers against yours. You notice the scrape of the rough patches of skin around her knuckles, but you don't mind, because you're feeling safe and loved as the two of you sit quietly together.

The vivid nature of this dream proves it as a visitation from Spirit. The colors, the feel of the wind and of Grandma's hand in yours, and the overwhelming sense of security are markers indicating its veracity. A true visitation will be an event always remembered by the living, and we recall certain scenarios because our physical senses are heightened and stimulated in a way that makes them impossible to forget. Of course, this is a good thing—we don't want to forget our encounters with Spirit!

One thing to remember: a negative dream experience with a passed-over loved one is the mind's way of processing emotion. If you dream of your deceased grandmother and you're having a heated argument, this is *not* a visitation. This is your psyche sorting out issues that you may harbor with Grandma and helping your mind to process through them. A dream visitation from Spirit is never a negative experience; it is healing for both parties.

You can ask for Spirit to visit you in your dreams. Before going to sleep at night, take a few deep breaths, close your eyes, and invite your spirit people to come into your dreams. Set the intention in your mind that you are ready and open for this to happen, and do not harbor any doubt that it will. Be sure to keep a pen and paper handy on your nightstand so that as soon as you wake up, you can jot down any dreams you've had. If you wait until after your morning trip to the bathroom or your first cup of coffee, most likely you'll begin to forget your dreams, so be sure to write down your impressions before you even get out of bed. And don't give up if you don't remember a visit the first time you ask for one. Sometimes it takes several days or weeks before you can open yourself up enough to receive a blessing like this from Spirit. If you're consistent and committed to it, though, a visit will occur.

These are just some of the ways that Spirit may choose to communicate from their vantage point on the Other Side. Communications are as unique as the souls that send them, so be alert and in tune with the world around you so you don't miss what your loved ones are saying to you!

I swear that every day, the framed photo I have of my dead brother has moved. I think this may be a message from him. Am I crazy?

The easiest way to determine if this is a message is to ask yourself some sensible questions. First, is there any other way the picture could have moved? Did your husband rearrange the photo and its neighbors while dusting the bureau? Do you have a cat that could have bumped into the photo frame while prowling about, thus moving it to another spot? If you're not sure, place a piece of blank paper underneath the frame in its normal resting place. Take a pen and draw an outline around the base of the frame so that if you picked it up, you could still see the outline of where the frame should be. Then, wait and see what happens. If the movement is obvious enough for you to notice it, you'll definitely be able to tell if the frame moves again by how far off the inked outline is. If it turns out that your photo is indeed moving, smile and thank your brother for the message, because he definitely wants you to know he's thinking of you!

Do my loved ones hear my thoughts when I think about them? Do they hear my prayers when I pray for them?

Because so much of the energy of the Other Side is driven by thought vibrations, their potency is much more palpable and powerful to our spirit friends. They do hear the thoughts that we direct to them, and they're able to respond to these if they need to do so. For instance, if I were to ask my mother in Spirit to help with an issue concerning my children, I know that she would instantly be aware of my request, and she would do what she could from her place in the afterlife to aid my boys. This might be something as simple as sending a thought of love to the them, or bringing smiles to their faces or a sense of relief to them in a time of stress. It might be that she would say extra prayers for their situation, for our loved ones do pray to Creator on the Other Side, just as we pray here. Or she might be able to do something more physical and tangible, such as help them find books they need at the library for a school assignment. If you send a thought to a loved one, be assured that your loved one does sense and understand it.

Prayers are a slightly different matter. Our loved ones don't eavesdrop on our private prayer conversations, which are entered into in a sacred space of love and intimacy with Creator that no one can disrupt. If we pray for them, however, they feel the energy of those prayers, which help to uplift, inspire, and heal them in their place in the spirit realms. This feeling is unique to the energy of prayer, and these souls do recognize then that someone has prayed for them, and they're extremely grateful for the loving energy that is thus directed to them.

One of the best things we can do for our loved ones is to pray for them, especially just after they've passed over to the Other Side. Asking Creator, the angels, and their spirit guides that they undergo a speedy, easy, and happy transition helps to make the passage from this world to the next smoother, and it helps the newly arrived to acclimate faster to the afterlife.

What kinds of things can my loved ones help me with from the Other Side?

Our spirit family and friends can help us with many issues. The challenge for us is realizing when they're sending the assistance and guidance we've requested! It's important to understand that when we ask for aid, we always receive it, but we may miss it because we're not confident that we'll get what we need, and we may not be open to the signs and messages that Spirit sends. When I first began working with spirit energies, I wanted to believe that I could receive help, but I harbored a great deal of doubt. This doubt set up a negative auric field around me, which attracted more negative energy, compounding my low self-esteem and my fear of failure. I'm sure my spirit friends were trying to help me, but they couldn't break through the cloud of negativity enveloping me. When I finally began to believe in myself as a divine being with a right to assistance, I was able to open myself up more to receive it, and I started noticing the wonderful things that were happening to me.

Over time, I also learned to be very specific about my requests to Spirit so that I would be able to measure the success of my communications. Several years ago, I wanted to leave my job at a department store spa to open my own practice. I dreamed of an office space where I could treat my massage-therapy clients, as well as do private readings for mediumship and Tarot clients. I worried, however, that I wouldn't be able to afford an office in an area of town close to my clientele. And, naturally, the prospect of being my own boss thrilled me and terrified me at the same time.

After several weeks of agonizing over this, I finally said to Spirit, "OK, look. If this is the right decision for me, send me three signs that I should leave my job at the spa and go out on my own. And I need them by the end of the week, because I don't want to keep thinking about this." I set this intention on a Monday. That evening, my husband came home from work and said, "So-and-so's wife goes to a massage therapist, and he's looking for an office partner. Maybe you should call him."

I eyed my husband suspiciously, wondering when he'd become a mind reader, because I hadn't said anything to him about leaving my current job. He shrugged and replied, "I just thought maybe you should get out on your own." I took this as Sign #1 from Spirit and had my husband call his friend at work to get the number of the therapist. We set up a time to meet.

The day of the meeting, as I got ready, I said to Spirit in my mind, "Oh, by the way, this office needs to be affordable. The rent has to be less than $200 a month, or I won't be able to do it." Even as I set this intention, my practical side laughed. How was I ever going to find a space that cheap? I wondered if I wasn't setting myself up for failure on purpose, or maybe as some sort of snotty challenge to Spirit, but I grabbed the car keys anyway and headed to the building where the new office was located.

The therapist, whose name is Larry, greeted me and showed me around the office space. It was clean and neat, with a bathroom in the hallway and a small reception area where clients could wait. The room that would be mine faced the street, but it was fairly quiet, with enough space for my massage table, accessories, and a tiny sitting area for reading clients. Larry and I chatted for a while about massage theory and our training, and although he was much more sports-oriented than me, I felt we would get along fine. The one question in my mind was whether he'd be open to me doing energy work and readings along with massage. I took a deep breath and asked him, expecting him to run screaming from the room.

He gave me a cool, assessing look for a moment and then said, "So, you're a psychic?"

"Yes," I replied. "I've been doing this kind of work for a long time, and I'd like to incorporate it into my practice. Would that be a problem for you?"

"Nope," he said shortly, and that was the end of that. I took his easy answer as Sign #2 from Spirit, breathed a sigh of relief, and stood up to go.

"I'd like to think some more about it," I told him, shaking his hand again. "When do you need an answer?"

"I'd really like to have someone by the end of the week," Larry replied.

"That's fine." I moved to the door and was about to open it when he stopped me.

"Geez, I almost forgot to tell you. The rent. It's $163 a month, plus about $10 for the phone bill."

I stopped dead in my tracks. "Did you say $163?" I was dumbfounded. It was a nice part of town, near almost all of my existing clients, on a major thoroughfare. "Are you sure?"

"Yeah. I got a great deal from the landlady. It's a real steal."

Sign #3. I felt like Spirit was hitting me upside the head with a two-by-four. I grinned and took a step back into the room. "On second thought, I don't need any more time to think about it. Where do I sign?"

Do you see just how much Spirit can help you if you ask for intercession? Believe me, that was a lesson for me in listening and acting on Spirit's advice and guidance. And, just for the record: Larry was my office mate for the next five years or so, and I learned a lot from him. We parted only because he no longer wanted to maintain a separate office from his practice at a local sports club. I'll always be grateful to him for giving me a chance, and to Spirit for helping me when I needed it.

You can do the same thing in your life when making decisions or planning goals. Remember the example where you asked your spirit guide to help you affirm her name by showing you three irises? You can use a similar task when asking for guidance about life issues from your loved ones. Ask your mother to show you three roses if she approves of your new boyfriend, or ask your uncle to show you three stars if he thinks your finances are in a good place to plan a vacation. Be alert to how these may show up in your life: as pictures in books or magazines, on television, in song titles, on the street, at your job, or any other way. And if they don't come into your life, perhaps your loved one wants you to rethink that idea or decision. Remember, always, that it's up to you—it's your life, and your free will must dictate how you'll live it. But if you ask for feedback, guidance, or help from Spirit, you *will* receive it.

I keep thinking I see someone out of the corner of my eye.
When I turn and look, no one is there. What does this mean?

Spirit communication is controlled by the Natural Law of Vibration, which tells us that all matter vibrates. In Spirit, our loved ones and guides are pure energy. Their vibrations are much higher than ours, since ours consist of physical matter. Because the spirit world is all around the physical world, penetrating and overlapping this plane of existence, we'll sometimes notice flashes of movement that indicate the presence of a spirit. That spirit, whether it's a loved one of ours, a guide, or a complete stranger, is passing by in whatever plane that spirit currently occupies in the afterlife, but, for some reason, his energy slows just enough for a split second to make him visible to an aware observer. Thus, we may notice the movement, but when we turn to look at it with keen eyes, the image is gone. Many times, this is one of your guides or a loved one hanging around, letting you know that they're present in your life. You aren't imagining things!

Once in a while, out of the blue, a song or a portion of song lyrics will
play over and over in my head for days or even weeks. Could Spirit be
trying to send me a message?

Definitely! Remember that most spirit contact is mind-to-mind communication, and if your spirit loved ones have something to tell you, they can use any and all means to deliver the message. Repetitive thoughts and words are an easy way for Spirit to bring through a meaningful message, because it's easy for Spirit to impress these upon our minds. Song lyrics are especially popular because many of us get songs stuck in our brains—the key is to recognize when it's just a routine brain glitch and when it's a message. If the same song plays over and over and over in your head, more than likely it's been implanted there by a spirit being for a reason. Listen to the words of the song and analyze them. There may be a message hidden in the lyrics.

Imagine that you're worried about your friend who is scheduled to undergo knee surgery in a few days. She tells you her plans on the telephone, and you wonder if she's made the right decision about her health. The next morning, you wake up with the song "Walking on Sunshine" stuck in your head. Eventually it goes away, but later in the afternoon, when you're daydreaming about your friend again, the song lyrics start up in your mind. Throughout the evening, you hear snatches of the music in your head, and you notice that they seem to come when you're considering your friend's situation. It's not a coincidence that this is happening! You realize that someone in Spirit (maybe even your friend's mother, who passed away earlier in the year) is trying to send you a message about a positive outcome for your friend. By analyzing the song lyrics, you determine that your friend has nothing to worry about in her upcoming surgery, and this is Spirit's way of reassuring you (and her, if you pass the message along) that she has nothing to fear. Isn't it amazing how Spirit can use these methods to support us in our everyday lives?

How do I know whether the taps I hear or the little flashes of light I see are just some sort of physical glitch, my imagination, or Spirit trying to communicate?

It's important to remember that not everything that happens in life is a message from Spirit. Sometimes the den lights waver because of a storm, or the house settles, producing creaks in the floorboards or rattles in the walls. Human beings are very inventive, imaginative creatures, and it's hard for us sometimes to separate reality from fantasy. Spirit can, however, manipulate physical objects, which makes these types of connections a little more substantial and therefore believable for some of us. But how do you really know if it's true or not?

Several years ago, a wonderful member of my church passed away. Theresa was an older lady when I met her, but she was an enthusiastic and energetic participant in our church community from the day she first began attending services, and she plunged into our Mediumship Training Program with gusto. She told me she'd always wanted to do spirit work, and she certainly wasn't going to let age stop her. She was well on her way to becoming an excellent medium when she fell ill, and unfortunately for all of us, she passed into Spirit before she could complete her mediumship and ministerial training. Theresa was an inspiring woman; she proved to me again and again the importance of following your dreams and overcoming obstacles and challenges that appeared. I felt honored to know her, and I was deeply saddened by her loss.

On the day that Theresa passed away, I went into my kitchen to get something to drink. I'd been up late the night before, praying the rosary for Theresa and her family, and I'd just received word from another minister at my church that she'd passed away. I stepped into the kitchen and flipped the light switch, still thinking of my friend. The overhead light came on, but then it flickered and went out completely. I couldn't understand it—the fixture wasn't brand-new, but the bulb was less than a few months old, and we'd had no problems with it up to that point.

I toggled the switch up and down, but the room remained dark. I frowned, but then Theresa's death flooded back into my mind. I felt her presence, as tangible and as real as if she'd been standing there in her physical body, pressing on my skin and making the hairs on the back of my neck rise. I wasn't scared—I'm way beyond fear like that at this point in my life as a medium—but my mind was still processing everything. Finally, I looked up at the light fixture in the middle of the ceiling and whispered, "Theresa? Is that you?" As soon as the words left my lips, the fixture flickered again and came on, flooding the kitchen with light. I smiled, because I knew this was Theresa's way of thanking me for all my prayers. She'd made her transition to the Other Side, and she wanted me to know she was doing fine.

Now, I'm sure some people would chalk this experience up to a glitch in the wiring of my house or my overactive imagination. I've found, however, that you need to trust your instincts and your feelings in cases like these. If you've been thinking about the spouse you just lost and you feel something press into your shoulder, something that feels very much like his hand, then how can you dispute that it's real? How can you ignore it, or choose to believe that it's not a message from your beloved but a flight of fantasy instead? If you smell the perfume that your mother always wore while you're remembering a funny situation from your life with her, isn't it plausible that she realized you were thinking of her and wanted to confirm to you that she's aware of your thoughts?

I'm not going to be able to convince you of the continuation of life after death if you're determined not to believe in it. But if you can at least open your mind to the possibility, if you can accept that energy cannot be destroyed and so must continue on in some capacity, and if you believe that your deceased friends and family are capable of exceptional amounts of love, then maybe you can experience something that will persuade you to believe in their ability to communicate from the Other Side. Ask yourself if the communication seems reasonable. If you're not intoxicated or distraught at the time, it's not your mind playing tricks. It's real. You trusted your loved ones in life, didn't you? Why not trust them now?

If Spirit wants to talk to you, why don't they just call your name instead of giving some obscure information?

Well, sometimes they *do* call your name. Have you never had the experience of hearing your name called, turning around, and seeing no one? I've had this happen to me many, many times, and for years I thought I was imagining it. When I started studying as a medium, however, I realized that my guides and loved ones had been trying to get my attention by calling my name, but I hadn't understood that they could do that. Now when I hear my name called, I pay attention, because there's usually a message that follows that initial contact.

Sometimes Spirit talks to us symbolically, which may be confusing to those unfamiliar with this shorthand language. The reason Spirit uses symbolism during contact is because it's easier for Spirit to communicate this way rather than trying to spell an entire message out word for word, letter for letter. For instance, your deceased brother may want you to know how much he loves you. Instead of yelling in your ear, "Hey, Sis, I love you," a task that requires inordinate amounts of energy, he may touch your mind with his thoughts and send you a picture of a red rose. You may suddenly think of him and see the rose in your mind, but you might not put the two together unless you know that roses are symbolic of love. A study of symbolism may help you to recognize simple messages that Spirit may try to impart.

You can also ask for your spirit people to send you specific signs, as we've discussed before. Ask your retriever-loving aunt to show you pictures of dogs, or petition your gardener-nephew to send you butterflies when you're outdoors. If you're diligent about asking and are open to perceiving them, these types of requests do work.

My grandfather's been dead for ten years. Why hasn't he ever come through to me?

There could be several reasons why you've not heard from your grandfather. The most obvious is that he's tried to contact you in some of the ways mentioned above but you've not been aware of his presence or his attempts at communication.

Ask for a tangible sign from Grandpa, be consistent about it, and see what happens. He may get in touch very soon.

From the spirit side of life, Grandpa might be experiencing many different things that inhibit his ability to communicate. Even though he's been gone a decade, it's important to keep in mind that time doesn't exist on the Other Side. Ten years seems like a long time to us, but to Grandpa, his time in Spirit may be like the blink of an eye. He may still be acclimating to his new home. He may not be aware yet that he can communicate, or he may not be listening to his guides, teachers, and loved ones over there that can help him to re-learn the communication process. He may simply be unwilling to make contact—not because he doesn't love you, but perhaps because he has other things he wants to do, learn, see, and experience. These factors can all influence whether or not he's gotten messages through. Again, sending thoughts to him that you'd like to hear from him may help him to realize that contact from him is important to you.

If someone died generations ago, can she still communicate from Spirit? Will she stop communicating at some point?

The answer to this question really depends on the individual spirit involved. I've had plenty of spirits that passed away twenty, thirty, forty, or even fifty years ago come through in readings for clients. As we've mentioned before, there's no time in Spirit, so a soul can stay on the Other Side—learning, growing, and communicating—for as long as she wishes to do so. It's all up to the soul and what she chooses to experience during her time in the afterlife.

I would be remiss if I didn't tell you, though, that it does appear that some spirits communicate for a while from the Other Side, and then the contact with them begins to taper off. From a personal standpoint, I've noticed this with my mother, who made her transition in the year 2000. For the first couple of years after she was gone, she contacted me quite frequently, sending messages through other mediums, through dreams, and through my own experiences. Nine years later, however, the communications from her have dwindled to far fewer than before.

When I asked my spirit guides to explain this, Merlin, my master teacher, told me that she has become very involved in her own projects and studies that occupy most of her time, and although she still thinks of my family and sends us love and prayers, she is concentrating now on her soul's progression, which is important for all of us as spiritual beings. Of course, I understand this and wish her nothing but the best— but I'd be lying if I told you I didn't miss the contact. Still, I content myself with the fact that she's achieving what she needs to as a soul, and I know I'll see her again when I make my transition to the Other Side. I do believe, however, that my mom still intercedes when I ask her for help, and that she still hears me when I talk to her. But I don't feel the need to ask specifically for messages from her any longer because my heart has healed from the grief of her passing. I miss her, yes, but I don't need to solicit contact with her all the time. There is comfort in the fact that I'll see her again and that our love for each other remains strong.

I don't believe souls purposely stop communicating from the Other Side unless they become too involved in other projects in their afterlife experience. They remain aware of their living loved ones and still understand what's going on in the physical realm. If they choose to reincarnate, however, I do believe the communication with them from the spirit planes ceases. We'll discuss reincarnation and its repercussions in the chapter entitled "Reincarnation and Other Lifetimes."

My wife recently passed away. How long will it take for her to come through in a reading or with a message for me?

Again, this is a very individual thing—hard to predict because of the unique experience of each soul. I'd say a good rule of thumb is to wait six months before seeking a connection through a professional medium, but if you're open and ask for contact, you may personally feel her presence much sooner than that. Try some of the suggestions for seeking contact in dreams or through everyday situations, and see if you sense her presence or a message from her. Don't become frustrated or give up if you don't receive anything right away. Give her some time to get settled on the Other Side, and keep trying. If you're diligent about contacting her, she will hear your thoughts and concerns about her, and eventually she'll be able to respond.

I've been asking and asking for a message from my father, but I haven't received one. Why?

If your dad's been gone less than a year, it may be that he's still acclimating to his new reality on the Other Side. It's fine to keep concentrating on achieving contact, but don't become frustrated or assume he doesn't care about you if you don't receive a message right away. If it's been over a year since your dad's transition, you may need to evaluate your own state of acceptance about his death. If you're still grieving exceptionally hard, you could be missing the message he's trying to send to you because of your distracted state of mind. Consider counseling or a grief support group to help you with your own healing process. It's much easier to clear the mind and make contact with the Other Side if you're in a peaceful state. If you feel strong emotionally, try asking for specific contact, as described in the sections regarding dreams or signs from Spirit. Remain as open and receptive as you can to contact by practicing the meditations in this book (see the appendix for help) and by praying and honoring your own divinity. If you still can't seem to find a connection to your dad, you may want to seek the help of a professional medium, who can possibly bring him through in a reading or coach you in person to achieve your own sense of his presence in your life.

I'm very concerned about some issues with my father's will, but when he came through in a reading I had, he didn't even talk about that. He spoke instead about some incident from my childhood. Why didn't he talk about the will? Is he even aware of the problems that I'm having?

First and foremost, spirits come through in readings or with messages in order to send loving greetings to us. They want us to know how they're doing in their new life and to reassure us that they haven't forgotten us. As much as they can know about our current life situations, they may not speak about them because their job is not to give us direction and guidance. They may offer advice at times, but many of the souls that have crossed over have moved beyond the concerns of the physical world. Of course, they do care that we might be worried or stressed about an issue—they still love us; that hasn't changed. They may recognize, however, that facing challenges is important to our growth process, and so they may choose not to address these issues so that we may work them out ourselves. I always recommend that people ask their spirit guides, teachers, and angels for advice and guidance about life matters. Our guides have taken on those roles in order to advance and learn, too, and angels have been commissioned by Creator to aid us. Let them do their jobs, and let your loved ones relax and concentrate on their own advancement once they've crossed over. And trust that all is in Divine Order; your problems will work out, especially if you ask for the highest and best outcome for everyone involved.

My grandfather died at the age of ninety, but when he came through in a reading, he appeared to be much, much younger. Is this possible?
Remember that, in the afterlife, our loved ones have no tangible body. They are pure energy, and they usually send messages to us through mind-to-mind communication. If your grandfather sent you a picture in your mind where he appeared to be much younger, he may just prefer how he looked at the age of thirty to his appearance when he passed away. I've seen many spirits come through in readings assuming the age when they felt most comfortable and confident. For many of us, this is usually from our late twenties into

our early fifties. Often, our loved ones are trying to let us know that they are whole again. They feel good, vibrant, and healthy on the Other Side, and appearing younger is one way to convey that message.

My parents divorced when I was young, but my father came through in a reading and wanted to give a loving message to my mother. What's that all about?

Perhaps your father has learned something about forgiveness and the many levels of love in the afterlife. Just because he and your mother did not stay together in the physical world doesn't mean their relationship wasn't productive or important to their spiritual progression as souls. You may never know what your dad's lessons were while he was in the body, and it's really not important—they're his lessons, and you have your own. Many spirits, however, come to a broader and more ecumenical understanding of themselves and others that have shared their lives when they undergo their life review after making their transitions. Maybe your father was trying to let your mother know that he appreciated her presence in his life; maybe he wanted to tell her he was sorry; maybe he wanted to pass on forgiveness for hurts that she caused him. Love takes many forms, and when we can move past anger, hurt, resentment, and other negative emotions from failed relationships, we enter into a more positive energy, which helps us to progress spiritually. It sounds like this is what's happened to your father on the Other Side, and it's really wonderful that he's reached this spiritual understanding.

I really wanted to hear from my sister in a reading, but my great-aunt Flo came through instead. I didn't even know her—she passed away before I was born. Why would she come through and my sister wouldn't?

It's always a good idea to go into a reading with an open mind about who may come through from the Other Side. Just because you didn't know Great-Aunt Flo doesn't mean she doesn't know you! She knows who her family is, and she may have an important message to impart to you. She may also be acting as a spokesperson for your entire family in the afterlife. Perhaps your sister wasn't able to be present for your reading; she may have had another engagement (yes, this happens), or she may have been entrenched in her studies or activities there. If she's new to the spirit world, she might not yet be familiar enough with the communication process, so she may have relied on another member of the family (Flo) to come through in your reading with greetings. If it's really important to you to hear from your sister, try some of the exercises already mentioned to initiate contact with her. Nevertheless, it's always a blessing when Spirit comes through in a reading. It may be disappointing not to hear from the person you really miss and want to connect with, but remember that all spirits are working hard to get a message through to you. Try to have an appreciation and some respect for that process.

My uncle Fred came through in my reading to give me advice about my business. When he was alive, he went bankrupt three times. Should I listen to him?

Here's something really important to keep in mind when communicating with loved ones and their energies in Spirit:

no one becomes instantly enlightened and all-knowing when he makes his transition. Some folks seem to believe that a spirit may know better what you should do because he possesses some inside information that he gets from his position in the spirit world. This is not always the case. Souls retain the personality of their most recent incarnation when they pass into Spirit. If Uncle Fred was a poor businessman when he was here on the earth plane, he may not be the best advisor now that he's crossed over. Yes, he might have a broader understanding of spiritual concepts, and he may have learned a great deal since his transition, but it's been my experience that this happens in the realms of progression and enlightenment rather than in more mundane pursuits like business or finances. These areas of life are surely important to us, and it's fine for our spirit loved ones to comment on them and give their opinions. Remember, though, that they are opinions. You have to decide whether you believe the guidance provided is worthwhile, or if Uncle Fred is off his game.

I can relate to this myself. My mother adored my husband, Keith. He was definitely the apple of her eye and could do no wrong. And she was devoted to keeping him happy and well-fed, like the good German-Hungarian girl that she was.

Mom always baked a cake for my birthday. One year when Keith and I were still dating, she made me a chocolate cake with chocolate icing. Although I love chocolate, I was puzzled. My favorite cake is yellow with caramel frosting, my mother's specialty. When I asked her why she'd baked the chocolate one instead, she answered, "It's Keith's favorite."

"But Mom," I sputtered, exasperated. "It's *my* birthday!"

You get the picture.

My point is this: let's say I'm having a disagreement with my husband, and I go to get a reading to gain some perspective about it. My mother comes through, and she communicates that she thinks my husband is absolutely right about the situation, and I should definitely give in to whatever he wants. Because I know my mother's personality and her behavior when it comes to my husband, I would take that advice with a grain of salt. Mom always sided with Keith when she was here, and, because she retains her personality, she's most likely siding with him again for those same reasons. I need to listen, yes, but I also need to weigh her words against what I know about her and make my own decision based on what I think is right. You should do the same, when it comes to Uncle Fred and his business suggestions.

How do we know that spirits on the Other Side aren't lying? Do they have to tell the truth?

This is a complicated question with a complex answer. It's my understanding that every soul on the Other Side must tell the truth to the best of her ability and in tandem with her spiritual progression. Obviously, truth is what we're striving to achieve, support, and uphold as spiritually evolved beings. But what is truth? And when is it appropriate to bend that truth in order to support an even larger agenda of love? I'm sure all of us are guilty of telling at least little white lies in our current lives: "Oh, yes, I love your new hairstyle." "No, the roast doesn't taste burnt at all." "What a beautiful picture you painted for me!" To most of us, these white lies are harmless, because they spare the feelings of someone we care about. Why upset a loved one if we really don't mind chewing on the charred edge of our pot roast?

I'm not insinuating here that it's OK for a spirit to lie, nor am I suggesting that our loved ones come through and tell us little white lies to spare our feelings or to make a hard truth easier to confront. What I am saying is that some spirits, because of where they are in their own spiritual progression, may not be able to completely tell the truth all the time. Perhaps this is a lesson for someone, one that she's carrying over to her time in the afterlife, and it's one she's working diligently on in a place where her guides can help her even more effectively.

We must also face the brutal fact that some souls were liars here in the physical world, and they'll spend their time in the afterlife in a plane of existence that is best suited to that energy of deceit. There will be teachers there to help them progress past their challenges, but only if the soul herself wishes to advance. If a spirit comes through to speak to you that had a problem telling the truth in life, there's no reason to assume that she's improved since her transition. You can hope for her and send prayers that she'll learn her lessons about honesty, but I wouldn't advise trusting all of her messages.

Our guides and teachers are a completely different story. I've never had any reason to doubt that my guides are telling me anything but the truth. They may not be able to reveal everything to us—sometimes, we need to allow events and situations to unfold in their own divine time—but your guides are only interested in your progression. Lying to you serves no purpose other than to lower the energetic vibration. What spiritual guide would purposely do something like that?

How do we know that spirits who claim to be historical figures aren't tricksters or mimics?

Here's a very good rule of thumb when you're communicating with the spirit world: unless you knew John Lennon, Groucho Marx, or Princess Diana personally while they were in the body, or you're a member of their families, these souls more than likely aren't going to speak to you in a communication from Spirit. Why would they want to talk to someone they've never met before when they've got friends and family of their own? If you had an opportunity to make one phone call (like in the movies when a character gets arrested), wouldn't you choose to call someone close to you rather than a complete stranger? So if you've got a spirit coming through to you who claims to be President John F. Kennedy, more than likely you're either misunderstanding the communication, or that spirit is pulling your leg. (See the above question about lying spirits.)

The exception to this rule is the presence and the communication from very highly evolved energies called Ascended Masters. Ascended Masters are sometimes historical figures of great renown, such as Jesus, Buddha, or the Virgin Mother Mary. These beautiful beings will approach and communicate with anyone who is open to receiving their energies.

Many of us feel overwhelmed and perhaps unworthy of this type of communication. I myself used to be very uncomfortable with the idea that one of these Ascended Masters might want to work with me. I felt I didn't deserve this kind of attention. I realize now that I had not grown enough as a spiritual entity to understand my own inner divinity, which connects us to all of creation and links us directly to God. Until I could love and embrace my true self—a reflection of Creator and a divine being in my own right—I couldn't accept the idea that I could have direct communications with Jesus or any of the other Ascended Master energies. Now that I recognize and rejoice in my own divinity, this communication is available to me at any time, and it can be available to you, too. These amazing Ascended Masters want to work with all of us, to help us to reach our highest potential. If you're comfortable with your own divine essence, then you may receive messages from the Ascended Masters. Listen and meditate on what they have to share with you, and trust what you're receiving.

One note here: some people have masters or other guides working with them who may have "famous" names. For instance, my master guide is called Merlin, and many people have asked me if this is *the* Merlin who appears in Arthurian legend. My Merlin has explained to me that he is not *the* Merlin, but a disciple of that Merlin's energy, and so he calls himself Merlin to honor his own teacher. There is an Ascended Master Merlin as well, and this is the energy that the stories are based on. If your guide tells you his name is Thoreau, for example, he most likely is not the famous writer and thinker, but he may have been taught and influenced by that particular advanced soul.

Is it wrong to test the word of spirits?

Not at all! This question is even addressed in the Bible, in 1 John 4:1: "My dear friends, do not believe all who claim to have the Spirit, but test them to find out if the spirit they have comes from God" (*Good News Bible*). This is similar to the question above, but there are several other angles to explore here.

One important thing to consider in your communications is the energy that comes through from the spirit sending them. A trustworthy and loving spirit, whether it be one of your guides that you're getting to know or one of your deceased friends or family members, will always want the highest and best outcome for you. A positive entity will never try to convince you to do anything that will be harmful for you physically, emotionally, or spiritually. If, for instance, a spirit is urging you to lie about something, there may be no physical repercussions to this, but the lie could cause emotional harm to you or someone else, and it could retard your spiritual progression. If these types of situations are occurring in your communications, the spirit contacting you is a lower-vibration entity, and you need to end your association with him. Always set the intention in any communication that you initiate with Spirit for the highest and best information to come through, and it will, because only the highest and best entities will be able to deliver it to you.

As mentioned earlier, it's perfectly fine to ask your spirit guides and loved ones to do things for you that prove their good intentions. Ask them to arrange a table at a restaurant for you and your date, or ask them to help you get a parking space at a crowded event. As you work more and more with their energies, try asking them to predict the weather at a certain time on a particular date, or tell them to show you who will call you on the phone last before you go to bed at night. When you start to see that they're able to deliver accurate information about these subjects, you can begin to ask them for answers to questions in your own life that reflect your highest and best good. Working with Spirit in these ways helps to build trust and strengthens the connections between you.

Always trust your feelings when working with Spirit. Many people have a very highly refined sense of clairsentience (clear feeling, or impressional mediumship) and don't even know it. Clairsentience manifests as paying close attention to how you're feeling when meditating or communicating actively with Spirit. Most spirit contact brings a sense of calm, peaceful, loving energy. You may experience some excitement, like the feeling you get when you meet with a friend you haven't seen in a long time, but the energy vibration stays firmly anchored in love. If you're working with a spirit and you begin to feel apprehensive, fearful, or unbalanced, you need to end the communication and sort out your experience. Did you start to feel this way because you were uncomfortable with something your spirit contact communicated to you? Did the spirit herself make you feel overwhelmed or intimidated? Remember that you control spirit contact, and you're on equal footing with all spirit energies that may present themselves to you.

Just because a spirit is on the Other Side doesn't mean that he's better than you. Yes, an Ascended Master, or even a master teacher, may have journeyed further on his path of spiritual progression, but that doesn't mean he's more important than you are. And no evolved spirit being is ever going to make you feel that way! Trust the feelings—they mean something important, and you need to analyze them. Sometimes, we may feel out of sorts during a communication because we're having a bad day, our confidence is at a low point, we're emotionally exhausted, and so on. Only you can catalogue your feelings and determine if you were the reason the spirit contact felt weird, or if you were in contact with an energy that didn't belong with you.

If my mother came through in a reading once, will she come through in another reading? Will the medium recognize her?

Again, it's hard to predict who will come through in any sitting, but there's no reason to think that your mother won't communicate with you in a later reading. In fact, it may be easier for her to do so because, having successfully bridged the worlds before, she'll have a better understanding of how the process works from her end so that she can do it again. She may even be able to sustain the contact longer or more strongly in a subsequent sitting because of her familiarity and comfort with the process.

A medium may or may not recognize a specific presence as someone with whom she's communicated before. If the spirit makes a point of this information, the medium will bring it through because her job is to relay any and all messages as they're delivered. In my experience, I find it very hard to remember all of the sitters I've read for in the many years I've been doing this work. I'll have people come for another sitting a year or so after their initial one, and I simply won't recall anything about the original session, including the spirits that came through. I give too many readings to expect that I'll remember these kinds of details. Quite frankly, it amuses me when skeptics accuse mediums of remembering information from previous readings and feeding it back to their gullible clients. I have trouble remembering what day of the week it is, let alone whether Client A has a grandmother on her father's side of the family named Zelda who was born in Austria in 1925! How ridiculous!

I do, however, recognize certain energies of personal friends and family members, whether they're on the Other Side themselves or if I'm reading for them while they're still in the body. My father-in-law is on the Other Side, and while I never met him when he was alive, I feel I know his presence very well because he comes in quite often around my husband, my children, and my in-laws. He even appears often when I receive a personal reading from another medium. A colleague of mine lost her son several years ago, and all of the mediums we know seem to recognize his energy immediately when he comes through at a church service or in a circle where his mother is present. Some spirits are hard to forget, especially if you're around them quite frequently!

Can our deceased loved ones be with more than one living person at the same time?

In my research and experience, I haven't found or heard any references to this phenomenon. I have read many stories, however, about souls appearing to people at the moment of transition to say goodbye. Several cases of this are documented in the book *Hello from Heaven!* by Bill and Judy Guggenheim. Here's a similar example, sent to me by Candy B.:

> "My family had this . . . experience with my grandmother. She was very sick with cancer, and the week she died she made sure we took her back to her home. She spoke to almost all the family members and passed on her belongings.
>
> "One night, and I remember this even though I was nine at the time, my brother came running to my father and said that he saw an older woman passing by the bathroom door. Other members of the family said they felt her presence at that same instant. While my brother was telling us, the phone rang. My mother, who was caring for my grandma that night, was terrified because my grandmother had gone into cardiac arrest about five to seven minutes before. Mom had been trying to call but could barely dial since she was so nervous."

It seems that some spirits can appear to more than one person when they're making their transition, but the documentation for a true bilocation experience, during which a spirit would appear to more than one living person at the same time after she's been on the Other Side for a while, seems to be virtually nonexistent. Perhaps this is a phenomenon that souls might perfect at some point in the future through their studies in Spirit.

How can people in the spirit world come through to a medium who does not speak their native language?

As we've noted, most spirit communication takes place through a mind-to-mind link between the soul on the Other Side and the medium. Although a medium may be clairaudient and able to hear words and phrases that Spirit speaks to her, she may not be able to decipher terms in a language other than her own. This has happened to me several times when I've been delivering messages. Because my strongest spiritual sense is clairaudience, I've had folks come through who have spoken Hebrew and Russian to me. Unfortunately, I speak neither language, and I had no idea what they were trying to convey in their messages. In both cases, I was able to listen closely enough to the words the spirit said and repeated them to the person receiving the message. That person was then able to piece together what her loved one was trying to impart.

Although this was gratifying for me as the medium and meaningful for those who received the message, it's not an easy or fun way to work. This is where it's helpful if a medium can tune into her other senses of clairvoyance, clairsentience, or claircognizance to continue the conversation in a clearer way. A medium can ask the spirit to try to give her something else instead of words and phrases; she can ask the spirit to show her something, put something meaningful in her hand, draw a picture on a chalkboard, etc. She can ask that the spirit impress a sensation upon or within her body of how the spirit passed to the Other Side or of any medical issues the spirit had while still on the physical plane. All of these methods can be utilized to help a spirit deliver a message if language might be a barrier.

A friend who was terminally ill promised to send a specific sign to me when he reached the Other Side. So far, I haven't seen it. Why would he promise this and then renege?

I don't think your friend is purposely reneging on his promise. If you've read through the other questions in this chapter, I hope you understand the communication process better and realize why you may not have received a spirit message. Think about the following: how long your friend has been on the Other Side, the fact that he may have some emotional and spiritual healing to undergo, and the possibility that you may have simply missed the message if he already tried to send it to you. Meditating with the express purpose of reconnecting with him and asking him to remember to send his signal will most likely produce a happy result, especially if you're willing to pay close attention to the many ways the signal may come through.

Setting up a system like this with a loved one before either of you crosses over is not a bad idea. Keep it simple. Telling your husband that you'll send him a rose after you make your transition may seem very arbitrary, but it will be extremely meaningful to him when it happens. Another possibility is to agree on a specific word that you'll convey somehow from the Other Side. Choose something meaningful but uncomplicated. If you like hiking, maybe the word *backpack* or *mountain* is a good choice. This way, if you need to access your spouse through a medium from the afterlife, you can send the information in a variety of ways: by showing a picture of a backpack or a mountain, by spelling it out on a chalkboard, and so on. If you send the message directly to your husband, you can influence the magazine he picks up at the doctor's office, making sure he picks the one with a photo of Mt. Everest or an outdoor sports catalogue. This way, you'll be sure your loved one won't miss the sign you send.

Do our loved ones in Spirit miss us as much as we miss them?

Grief is one of the hardest challenges we face on the physical plane. Anyone who has lost someone close understands how devastating a death can be. It influences all aspects of your life, and it affects your physical, emotional, mental, and spiritual well-being. Recovering from the loss of a loved one is a very individual process, and some people move forward from their grief faster than others. Even when you finally feel that you're "over" the death, you still miss the physical presence of your loved one. You can't hug him, have an in-depth conversation with him, share a pizza with him, laugh with him, or any of the other things you enjoyed together. You continue to grieve, in a lesser way, forever.

Our loved ones who have crossed over to the afterlife do not experience grief when they arrive there. In fact, many describe the feelings of elation that envelop them when they make their transition. While those left behind in the physical world are steeped in grief, the soul that has died is immersed in joy. Many compare it to a homecoming party on the Other Side. This may not seem fair to those left behind who ache with sadness. Sometimes, it helps to focus on how much the spirit is gaining in the transition to the afterlife.

Remember, too, that there is no time in Spirit. Your loved one can make his transition, and to him, a reunion with you is only a few seconds away. For you, it may be years and years until you cross to the Other Side, and you may never stop missing him. But try to imagine how great the joy will be when you see each other again!

Do our loved ones miss us? Not in the same way we miss them, because they know that they'll see us again, that our souls will be together once more, and that very little time will pass until that happens. For them, the transition to the Other Side is a brand-new, wonderful beginning, and a return to an energy of love and bliss that is exciting and inspiring. They still love and remember us, and they'll be there when we finally come Home, too.

As you can see, our loved ones are very active in the spirit world, and they're eager and willing to stay in touch with us from their new vantage point on the Other Side. There, they experience healing and love that we in the physical world can't quite fathom, but it's an energy that we'll certainly recognize and remember once we make our transition to be with them again. And if we set our intention to keep in contact with them while paying attention to all of our senses and the world around us, we'll be able to keep our connection with our deceased loved ones intact. They'll never leave us as long as we remain open to receive the constant stream of love that they send.

RELIGION AND SPIRIT

Earlier in this book, I mentioned my hometown of Cincinnati and revealed some of the features that make it unique. One aspect of Cincinnati that I didn't mention is its very large Roman Catholic population. The following statistic may help you to understand just how prevalent Roman Catholicism is in my neck of the woods:

"Today in Cincinnati, Ohio, nearly one-fourth of school-age children in grades K–12 attend schools established and maintained by various Roman Catholic religious orders. Nationally the data is only 10 to 12 percent."[1]

I was a part of this community for a long time, studying in Catholic schools from first grade through my senior year

---

1. Thomas A. Kessinger, "Genesis of Catholic Schools in Southwestern Ohio" (2008). Online at www.allacademic.com (accessed August 31, 2009).

in high school, attending Catholic Mass every Sunday for the first eighteen years of my life, and even marrying in the Catholic Church. Most of my extended family, from distant cousins to in-laws, is Catholic. Even though I left the Church to study Wicca and eventually became an ordained Spiritualist minister, I still consider my Catholic upbringing and beliefs to be integral to who I am as a spiritual being. I believe very strongly in honoring the past, because it's an important stepping stone to where we're going and who we're becoming.

I mention this because Catholicism permeates my hometown's culture and the people who live here. Many of the clients I see in my massage therapy and clairvoyant reading practice are either Catholic or grew up in a Catholic household. About half of the people who attend my church's services come from a Catholic background. And many of these folks, who are interested in spirit communication and want to learn more about it, are terrified at first because they're afraid their curiosity will damn them eternally.

Catholics are not alone with this fear. The majority of Christians condemn spirit communication because of a few passages in the Bible that seem to reject it (we'll investigate those in a few moments). Many seem to think that spirit communication is linked in some way to communing with Satan. This notion reaches back hundreds of years to when many Pagan practices, like divination and herbal healing, were branded as evil by the ever-strengthening Church. In order to control the people and to impress the message of this new religion upon them, the Church elders attached stigma and sin to these practices, accusing those who supported them of terrible things. Over the centuries, many people were put to death as heretics when they refused to give up their practices or beliefs. The death sentences may have ended, but the stain of sin and evil still overshadows spirit communication in a large portion of Christian thought and doctrine.

My purpose in addressing religion is not to try to convince anyone to give up or change certain beliefs. Instead, I hope this chapter will give you a better understanding of why spirit communication may be scary to some people, how to address these concerns yourself, and which religions accept spirit communication as a part of their practices.

My family is very religious and believes my interest in spirit communication is evil. Do you have any advice?

Of all of the questions in this book, this is probably the one I hear the most. I believe the outrage that some people express about spirit communication is based on fear. If we're afraid of something, we tend to stay as far away from it as possible, and we attempt to keep our loved ones away from it, too. What could possibly be more frightening than death and all its trappings?

Well, as we've seen, death really isn't anything to fear. In order to alleviate the fear of death, however, you have to explore the possibilities of it, and this is something that many religious folks aren't willing to do. It might mean that their findings don't add up to what their religious institution has been preaching for years. This is a scary proposition, especially if they've invested a great deal of emotional, physical, and spiritual energy in a church or organization. Many religions don't advocate the concept of free thought, personal responsibility, or research to their followers. They insist instead on loyalty to the faith, often reinforced by intoning what dire consequences will occur if someone strays from the path.

So, yes: they're trying to scare you out of thinking for yourself and using your God-given gift of free will. That doesn't sound very spiritual to me.

That said, think about this: respect shown usually garners respect. If you respect your family's religious views, you're modeling the type of behavior you expect in return. If you present what you believe in a clear, unthreatening, educated manner, those who doubt it will give it more weight because you aren't afraid of questions and debate. Show them this book or others in the reference section and encourage them to read the compelling material written about after-death communication. Ask them if they've ever had a dream about a departed loved one that seemed real, and discuss with them how this could be a visitation. Explain to them how contact with a soul on the Other Side reflects the great love that individual still harbors for those left behind, and question how this could possibly be evil. If you're pleasant and calm during these exchanges, chances are your gentle approach will be matched in a similar way.

Don't become embroiled in a battle. If you're an adult, you can make your own choices, which includes structuring your personal belief system. If a debate ever becomes heated, take the higher road and simply say, "I can see that this discussion is upsetting you, and that was never my intention. I appreciate your concern for me, but we'll need to agree to disagree on this subject. Let's talk about something else." If the other person insists on yelling or becomes abusive, stay peaceful and remove yourself from the situation. Responding with anger, outrage, or sorrow only feeds into the negative energy. You don't need that. It isn't your job in life to convince anyone of anything. If there's one thing I've learned over the years, it's that faith is something that's unshakable and inarguable, and it's useless to waste energy trying to change a person's mind (as, ironically, he or she is trying to do to you). But you do have the right to be treated with respect. If you're not being shown that, you need to question whether the relationship is worth pursuing.

I'm a Christian, but I still believe in spirit communication. Is that OK? Where does Jesus fit into all of this?

Many Christians fear spirit communication because of several passages in the Old Testament of the Bible. These are mostly found in the books Leviticus and Deuteronomy, which contain extensive descriptions of what the Hebrew people were allowed or not allowed to do. For example, from Deuteronomy 18:10–12: " . . . and don't let them consult the spirits of the dead. The Lord your God hates people who do these disgusting things . . . " (*Good News Bible*).

The book of Leviticus states several times that communion with spirits is unacceptable, with the consequences becoming worse with every mention: ". . . you will be ritually unclean" (Leviticus 19:31); "I [the Lord] will turn against you and will cut you off from among your people" (Leviticus 20:6); "Any man or woman who consults the spirits of the dead shall be stoned to death" (Leviticus 20:27). From these passages, it seems that communication with the departed is something that made Yahweh furious.

However, consider some other things that were prohibited: in Leviticus 19:19, followers are told not to cross-breed animals (so much for Holstein cattle, some of the best milk producers in the world), to avoid planting two kinds of seed in the same field (nowadays used to develop disease resistance and to conserve land), and to never wear clothing made from two types of materials (forget about Spandex, ladies, and the wonders it can perform when we want to hide a few pounds). In our modern world, these directives may seem silly or illogical—but are they really as weighty in consequence as speaking to the dead?

Another consideration is that in the book of Leviticus, the following passage also appears: "If you need slaves, you may buy them from the nations around you. You may also buy the children of the foreigners who are living among you" (25:44–45). So . . . it's OK to buy and keep another human being in bondage, but wearing a blended fabric isn't? In Exodus 21:7, we learn that it's acceptable to sell your daughter either into slavery or to a man who wishes to marry her. Really? I know quite a few women, young and old, myself included, who would take issue with this. There are also many references to polygamy (such as in Deuteronomy 21:15–17) in the Old Testament, a lifestyle that has been outlawed in many cultures, including the United States. When you compare these kinds of passages, how can you know which are correct and which are not?

Some Christians believe the Bible to be the literal word of God, and that everything within it must be followed to the letter. Several passages, however, like stoning an adulterer (Leviticus 20:10, just to point out one reference), depict punishments considered outrageous in our world today. I'm not defending adultery; I'm simply pointing out that the "rules" dictated in many parts of the Old Testament seem arbitrary and, in some ways, illogical. And once you decide that one rule is foolish and unnecessary to follow, what's to say that the whole book isn't the same way?

My final, and perhaps most important, point: the Old Testament outlines some very dire consequences for the breaking of these rules—chiefly, that the culprit lose his or her life. We're also told frequently (as in the above-referenced passage) that the Lord hates people who act in a prohibited manner. I don't know about you, but the Creator that I understand is a loving, compassionate Presence. The Creator that I know does not condone hate in any form and is incapable of it. And the Creator that I have welcomed into my life certainly does not support the killing of any of His beloved children, no matter their mistakes. I cannot fathom a God of vengeance and venom like the one depicted so often in the Old Testament.

Now, let's talk about Jesus.

Jesus is believed by Christians to be the Christ, the promised Messiah sent by God to save His people. The Hebrews believed that the Messiah would deliver them from the many other countries and cultures that had oppressed them for hundreds of years. Jesus' message was that he hadn't come to free the Hebrews from their foreign rulers, but to save souls from sin and to assure people of life with him and his Father after death. True Christians model their lives after the behavior of Jesus Christ and follow the tenets that he outlined in the New Testament Gospels of Matthew, Mark, Luke, and John.

In examining what Jesus had to say as recorded in the Gospels, there are no passages that reflect a condemnation of mediumship or after-death communication. In fact, Jesus himself practiced communication with the spirit world, as evidenced in this quotation from Matthew 17:2–3:

"As they looked on, a change came over Jesus; his face was shining like the sun, and his clothes were dazzling white. Then the three disciples saw Moses and Elijah talking with Jesus."

The prophets Moses and Elijah had died many, many years before Jesus lived. Obviously, they were able to communicate with him from their places in the afterlife, perhaps even taking the roles of spirit teachers for Jesus. Jesus didn't seem to think this at all odd, although he warned his disciples not to tell anyone about the communication (perhaps he was afraid he'd be stoned, given the tenets of Leviticus). So Jesus himself was a medium, in the strictest sense of the word: he communicated with spirits.

Even more importantly, Jesus showed his followers that after-death communication was possible by contacting them after his own transition:

"Then Jesus came and stood among them. 'Peace be with you,' he said. After saying this, he showed them his hands and his side. The disciples were filled with joy at seeing the Lord" (John 20:19–20).

Just like in a mediumship reading today, Jesus gave evidence of who he was by showing the disciples his hands and side, where he'd been injured during his death. He conveyed a message, and his appearance brought great happiness to those that he visited. By appearing to his friends and loved ones, Jesus confirmed that life continued on after death, and that communication with him from his new place in the spirit world was entirely possible and not dangerous, deluded, or sinful.

So, with all due respect to the Christian religion: how can you call yourself a follower of Christ and yet doubt that Jesus could contact the dead or did himself communicate from beyond the grave?

Yes, I realize—to Christians, Jesus is the Christ, which gives him powers other mortal men do not possess. And so I'll leave this subject with the following quotation from the Gospel of John, chapter 14, verse 12:

"I am telling you the truth: those who believe in me will do what I do—yes, they will do even greater things, for I go to the Father."

If you believe in Jesus (and even if you don't, but you recognize Jesus' divinity as a truth paralleling our own divinity), then you can communicate with spirits. You can do this work, and you shouldn't fear it in any way. Jesus didn't.

My family doesn't believe in spirit communication. How can I convince them?

I asked this very same question many years ago, when I first started studying mediumship in a formal training program. I was terrified that my loved ones, especially my parents, would pronounce me crazy and would be disappointed or hurt by my actions. I was also afraid that, if my husband and I decided to start a family, my children might be singled out for ridicule by their peers if they discovered what I believed. The idea of hiding my thoughts, feelings, and beliefs seemed wrong to me; hypocritical behavior has never settled easily on my heart, which is one reason I left the Catholic Church in the first place. And many people want to share their excitement about their interests with others. I was no exception, but I was petrified that my fascination with mediumship would bring nothing but heartache.

You may be nodding here, finding yourself in a similar situation. I slowly began to realize that by believing myself to be vulnerable to negative attacks about my beliefs, I was energetically setting myself up for that very thing. Like energy attracts like energy—that's a Natural Law of the Universe that cannot be avoided. If you don't want negative energy drawn into your vibration, you must change your thoughts, and thus the energy around yourself, to more positive ones. I also started to understand that knowledge was a powerful ally. The more I knew about spirit communication, the easier it was to defend my belief in it. I began to read everything I could about mediumship, the spirit world, near-death experiences, channeled writings, and the like. I even read books and articles written by skeptics so I could see their arguments, understand their logic, and then find ways to challenge them back. I also tried keeping myself in a high, loving vibration, not an argumentative one, so that if I received questions or found myself in a confrontation, I felt calm, strong, and ready to answer without becoming upset. Debate can actually help you to understand your own beliefs better, making you and your faith stronger, as long as it's approached in a positive way.

As I said earlier: you can't change someone else's mind if they don't want to change it. Trying to convince your spouse, your children, your parents, or your friends that spirit communication is a reality is not up to you. If they're interested, fantastic. Share everything you can with them and encourage them to explore on their own. If they're not interested or think it's a silly pursuit, don't back down, but recognize that you may have to find other people who condone your ideas and can support you in this work. You can still maintain relationships with people who don't share your beliefs—plenty of interfaith marriages succeed all the time. But don't be a crusader. You don't want anyone telling you what to believe, do you? Put yourself in their shoes and be tolerant, respectful, and as loving as possible.

What religions do believe in positive spirit communication?
Several religions support and practice spirit communication.

Many Native Americans believe in and pursue relationships with spirit communicators, especially totem animals and spirit helpers (see the previous chapter entitled "Spirit Guides, Teachers, and Angels"). Some Native Americans perform special ceremonies in order to connect more fully with wise animal spirits. Many Native American tribes also have a unique relationship with the spirits of their ancestors. For example, the Sioux people believe that everything in nature has a spirit of its own, and all are interdependent. An individual's soul is reliant upon the natural spirits of the animals, the plants, the stones, the collective tribe of which he is a part—all weave an energy web throughout the world. Sickness and natural disasters are reflections of imbalances in the energies that must be corrected by shamans, who communicate with the spirits to bring them back into alignment.

Pagans and Wiccans honor ancestors and celebrate the ability to communicate with the spirit world. Samhain, also known as Halloween, is the sabbat holiday that commemorates this belief. Traditions may include creating sacred spaces where pictures of deceased loved ones are displayed and preparing dinner tables to include empty place settings for those who have passed away. In ceremony, the dead are invited to participate, and scrying (crystal or mirror gazing) may be employed in order to catch a glimpse of a beloved friend or to divine any messages sent from the world of Spirit. Many Pagans commune throughout the year with personal spirit guides and seek advice and guidance on a regular basis. All spirits, including nature elementals, are welcomed and treated with love and respect. Depending on the pantheon of gods and goddesses particular to their traditions, Pagans and Wiccans also communicate with these energies, seeking their aid in achieving goals in all areas of their lives.

Although traditional Judaism appears to frown on communication with the dead (mostly because of the same books of the Hebrew Bible that we discussed previously), Jewish esoteric traditions seem to take a different view. According to Rabbi Geoffrey Dennis, author of the book *The Encyclopedia of Jewish Myth, Magic and Mysticism*, a *maggid* is a spirit guide or angelic teacher. The maggid apparently is the personification of some higher attribute, like Wisdom or the Torah, and usually substantiates itself within a person, displaying its influence through automatic writing, speaking in tongues, or trance. The maggid appears to manifest due to intense study of scripture combined with mystical discipline or ritual.

About 84 percent of Japanese people follow the religions of Shinto and Buddhism. Followers of Shinto believe in the *Kami*, which are the deities of the religion, the spirits that sustain the people. They are generally beneficent and quite pervasive throughout the natural world. The Kami also appear as creative forces, as exceptional people, and as guardians of areas and clans. In Shinto, ancestors are deeply respected and worshipped. Nature is sacred and revered. One example of this is displayed in the ancient Japanese art of origami, or paper folding. These beautiful and intricate patterns and shapes are often left as offerings at Shinto shrines, and the paper used is never cut, in order to honor the tree spirit that gave its life to make the paper. Shrines are often erected to honor the divinity of a particular Kami that inhabits the natural space, and prayers and dances are offered in ritual to show love and respect. Altars are placed in private homes to honor particular Kami and to remember deceased loved ones. The Kami are very active in the lives of their Shinto followers.

Buddhism also respects the spirits of nature that permeate the land, the waterways, the foliage, and people. Mahayana and Tantric Buddhism recognize external spirits that compassionately try to help confused human beings. The messengers of enlightenment described in the Sanskrit language and writings are called *Dakas* and *Dakinis* (male and female entities), while the protectors of enlightenment are called the *Dharmapalas*. These ascended teachers, however, are far beyond the understanding and concepts of ordinary human beings and therefore do not interact with us in ways we can perceive.

Many types of divine or semi-divine beings serve as messenger spirits and guides in the Hindu religion. These gods or demigods may be petitioned for help in achieving all manner of goals. These beings may also appear without prompting to give guidance or messages. Most Hindus, however, rely not on spirit guides but on incarnated gurus (spiritual leaders) for direction concerning life lessons and purposes. These gurus may communicate in dreams and visions, especially if they are no longer in the physical body.

Islam allows its followers to communicate with the dead, especially when visiting gravesites. Recitation of the Qur'an (the Muslim holy book) and saying prayers for the deceased are common practices. Muslims may greet the dead and offer prayers, but they do not worship ancestors as some religions do. A few members of the Sufi sect may try to commune with the spirits of the deceased during these visits, but this practice seems to be extremely limited. Muslims do believe in the *jinn*, often seen as destructive or negative spirits. Prayers and recitations of the Qur'an help to keep these energies at bay.

Belief in after-death communication is a core tenet of the Spiritualist religion. Spiritualists rely on meditation and personal development techniques to hone their spirit communication skills and seek guidance from their spirit teachers and deceased loved ones on a regular basis. They recognize, however, that an individual is personally responsible for decisions and choices made and do not rely solely on the advice given from Spirit.

Even the Roman Catholic religion supports some practices that could be viewed as spirit communication. While discouraging its members from contacting deceased relatives through their own meditations or with the help of a medium, Catholicism does encourage its followers in devotions to the Virgin Mary, the mother of Jesus Christ, and the many saints canonized by the Church. Mother Mary has made many appearances to the faithful throughout the centuries, even in modern times. (For more information on this phenomenon, peruse the book *Searching for Mary: An Exploration of Marian Apparitions Across the U.S.*, by Mark Garvey.) Since Mary has obviously made her transition into the higher planes, would these appearances not be considered spirit contact? The Catholic Church may not call them such (and often, the Church remains silent about these visitations, with their authorities hesitant to comment on any "miraculous interventions" until thorough investigations have been conducted), but her appearances fit the criteria for spirit contact.

In addition, many Catholics petition different saints for help with everyday matters, from Saint Anthony, the patron of lost items ("Help me find my car keys, Saint Anthony!") to Saint Joseph, Jesus' earthly father, whose statue is often buried upside down in the front yard when selling a home. If we believe that our spirit guides and angels hear and help us when called upon, is it really any different to believe that Saint Anthony has lent a hand in the quick recovery of our car keys?

This is a sampling of the religions and belief systems that put faith in some form of spirit communication. Believing that human beings are not alone and have access to guidance from loving, enlightened beings isn't as strange as some people might think.

From this chapter, you see that spirit communication and religion are not mutually exclusive, nor do you need to give up belief in a particular religious tradition if you're interested in the spirit world. The purpose of religion is to seek answers about God, and to share experiences of God with others who possess similar thoughts and ideas. It seems, however, that religion often dictates doctrine established by human beings instead of encouraging free thought and will. To me, this runs in opposition to what Creator really wants for us. Is not knowledge, and its attainment, one of our chief pursuits as human and spiritual beings? Would not an institution that insisted we give up our own authority and squelched our sense of inner divinity be contrary to God's hope for us as souls?

Like everything else presented in this book, this is an issue you must decide for yourself. I've chosen to pursue communication with Spirit as a means to become closer to Creator because I believe in its validity and the positive results it garners in those it touches. To that end, I refuse to succumb to the lure of dogma in any religion and prefer instead to investigate on my own. As the English writer Eden Phillpotts said, "The universe is full of magical things, waiting for our wits to grow sharper."

REINCARNATION AND OTHER LIFETIMES

Reincarnation, the belief that the soul is reborn in a new body and returns to Earth after death, seems to be a hotly debated topic among spiritual seekers. To many people in the Western world, where this axiom is not as prevalent, reincarnation may appear to be nothing more than wishful thinking. Many religions and philosophies, however, do profess a belief in reincarnation, or at least theorize its possibility. Among these faith systems are Buddhism, Gnostic Christianity, Theosophy, Spiritualism, Paganism, Wicca, Kabbalistic Judaism, Hinduism, and Unitarianism. Although views on the details vary from one to another, these traditions include in their ideology the basic belief that we die, go to the Other Side, and can choose to be reborn into another body on the earth plane.

Furthermore, science is beginning to make great strides in proving that reincarnation is a feasible theory. The groundbreaking work of psychiatrist Dr. Brian L. Weiss, catalogued in his first book, *Many Lives, Many Masters,* and his numerous subsequent publications, documents first-hand accounts of past-life regression therapy that highlight the previous incarnations his patients lived. In many of these cases, these patients were helped through emotional traumas in their current lifetimes by accessing past-life memories, witnessing past-life events and relationships, and gaining insights into how those affected their current states. Maybe you can empathize with trying to overcome irrational fears. I know I can.

When I was a child, I was afraid of the dark. Even now, as an adult, I prefer to sleep with the light on in my bedroom if my husband is away. I don't mind admitting this, because the majority of human beings can relate to a similar fear. Some of the most common phobias include arachnophobia (fear of spiders—glad to see I'm not alone in this one), aerophobia (fear of flying), claustrophobia (fear of being trapped in a small space), and necrophobia (fear of dying, the dead, or dead things—good thing I'm not afflicted with this, or it would make my work as a medium very difficult). Along with darkness and spiders, I also have to acknowledge my fear of heights (another common one called acrophobia). One phobia I no longer harbor, however, is nelophobia, more commonly known as a fear of glass—specifically, for me, broken glass. I was able to work through this fear, but it plagued me for many years.

A phobia of broken glass may sound like something that shouldn't be too hard to manage, but believe me, it wasn't easy. If you're the lucky individual who doesn't suffer from any phobias, you probably can't relate to the horrible sickening feeling of panic that descends when faced with your fear. Although I cringe over spiders, feel nauseated when I ride elevators to high places, and breathe more rapidly in dark spaces, the crushing sense of dread and terror that overwhelmed me when I saw broken glass is nearly impossible to describe. And it would pop up for me at the most unlikely times. While watching the action movie *Die Hard* with friends, I had to close my eyes and breathe deeply to keep from passing out after a barefoot Bruce Willis walked across a floor covered with shards of smashed window glass. My future husband nearly had to carry me out of my college apartment's kitchen after I dropped a juice glass, and froze when it shattered on the linoleum. And during a performance of a play, I nearly ruined an entire scene for all of the on-stage actors when I dropped the thermometer I was shaking, and could barely move when it broke at my feet.

To make matters worse, I had no idea why I reacted so badly to broken glass. I even asked my mother if she recalled any incidents from my childhood when glass had shattered and scared me, but she couldn't make connections to any such memories. I tried very hard to keep my responses calm, but the irrational anxiety seemed impossible to control. I assumed that this fear was something I would have to deal with my whole life.

The concepts of reincarnation and past lives immediately fascinated me when I discovered them in college. Using a guided meditation tape, I was able to tap into a memory of a past life as a wool worker in Ireland. Perhaps not a very exciting lifetime, but the experience led me to discover research indicating that phobias could sometimes be overcome by discovering the root of the fear through a past-life regression. Recognizing that this might help my fear of broken glass, I vowed to pursue past-life work if given the opportunity.

A few years later, someone in my husband's family told me that she was studying hypnosis, and I asked her if she did past-life regressions. When she affirmed that she did, I volunteered to be a guinea pig. She came to my house, armed with a cassette tape so we could record the session, and she described the process to me. She would use guided hypnosis techniques to help me enter an altered state where I could access my past-life memories and possibly understand better some of the choices, relationships, and emotions I carried forward from that lifetime into this one. I eagerly explained to her that I wanted to rid myself of the broken-glass trauma that seemed to be a terrifying and debilitating holdover from a previous incarnation. She was hesitant, having only done a handful of regressions, but if I was willing to try, so was she. I got comfortable on my massage table, and she began the regression.

Much of the process of that regression is lost to me, but several things I experienced remain etched on my mind as if the session happened yesterday. This family member purposely prompted me to recall the lifetime where I developed a fear that I wanted to overcome. In my mind, I immediately saw a lighthouse made of stone and glass standing on the rocky shore of a pounding, relentless sea. I knew with utter certainty that I was on the eastern shore of North America, very far north, probably in Maine or even Canada, sometime in the mid-1800s. The lighthouse was isolated but extremely important to the maritime industry along the coast, and I understood that I lived there with my father, the lighthouse keeper. I also understood without a doubt that my father was a dear friend of mine in my current lifetime, and that I was engaged to marry a sailor who had been gone at sea for quite some time. We were planning to marry as soon as he returned, and I realized that this soul is my husband in my current lifetime.

Just then, the scene changed. The waves swelled to dangerous sizes, and thick black clouds covered the seashore. Wind and torrential rain battered the lighthouse and the craggy rocks that surrounded it. I watched from inside the lighthouse windows as the storm worsened, my heart pounding as I frantically searched the horizon along with the sweep of the beacon. I knew my fiancé was out in that storm on his ship, and I was terrified he wouldn't make it back to land. A terrible cracking sound suddenly engulfed the roaring ocean and screaming wind, and the huge windows all around me imploded, showering me with broken glass. Fire sprang up from the wooden floor, and I realized the lighthouse had been struck by lightning. I ran down the spiraling stairs, calling for my father, and I emerged outside in the terrible storm. I huddled next to a rocky outcropping, screaming my father's name and crying as the lighthouse burned nearby. My father never came, trapped in the burning lighthouse, and I knew in my heart that my love was lost at sea, another victim of the brutal elements. I felt sick, lost, and abandoned.

I have no memory of my family member talking me through the regression, but I do recall a sense of peace finally settling over me. Through her prompting and gentle suggestions, I was able to release the fears I'd been carrying from that lifetime— not only the phobia of broken glass that I obviously associated with the terrible tragedy of losing my father and my fiancé, but the underlying fear I harbored of being abandoned by the people I loved. When the experience ended, I felt serene, and I was very pleased that I'd been able to connect with that past-life memory. Since then, broken glass has not bothered me in the least. The work that day also helped me to feel more worthy of the love that others give to me, and I understood my intense need for stability more when I realized it stemmed from being abandoned in that lifetime.

Some other interesting facts: in researching lighthouses from the mid-1800s, my family member and I discovered that many of them were constructed of stone and glass, just like the one I saw in my regression. The mechanism I'd seen used in the lighthouse to produce the beacon, which cast a doubt in my logical mind because it had looked modern to me, was introduced in the United States from France in the 1840s. It stands to reason, then, that this regression experience was real. I can certainly attest to how much it truly helped me to overcome some deeply seated fears.

Overcoming phobias is not the only reason to research past-life memories. Modern studies, done with people displaying physical marks and deformities, have linked these maladies to past lives in which that particular body part was negatively affected. In his book *Life Before Life*, Dr. Jim B. Tucker writes, "If . . . consciousness or mind can exist after the brain dies—if some part of us survives when our bodies die—and can enter a fetus to be reborn, then it follows that it can produce changes in the development of that fetus . . . Those (traumatic) memories could produce birthmarks or even birth defects that matched wounds that the mind had experienced in a previous life" (pp. 69–70).

Dr. Tucker goes on to document in his book many cases of children reborn who have physical conditions as well as memories that correspond to past lives they've led, situations and events that can be confirmed by family members and factual circumstances. Dr. Tucker's work continues today at the University of Virginia, where he directs this research at the Division of Perceptual Studies.

Another reason to explore past incarnations is to examine relationships from those lifetimes and how they may be affecting interactions with certain people in your current one. Many people recognize friends or family members when they experience a past life, and sometimes they may be able to discern important details about particular relationships that point to why the current liaison may be strained, broken, committed, obsessive, strong, abusive, and so on.

In interviewing folks about past-life experiences, my friend Donna described herself and her sister, Lynne, as very affectionate women, but, for some reason, neither of these ladies liked to hug the other. They were close and loved each other very much, but they couldn't bring themselves to embrace.

During a past-life regression experience, they discovered that they'd also been sisters in a lifetime in the early twentieth century, probably during the Depression, and they'd made some kind of raft to play on in a river. They were very young, probably between eight and ten years old, and once they got out on the water, they couldn't control the raft. It flipped over, casting the girls into the strong river currents, and the sisters drowned together—clutching each other in a terrified embrace.

Donna claims that once this memory was uncovered, she and Lynne understood why they were so afraid in this lifetime to hug. Why wouldn't they be, when their last memory of embracing that same soul was filled with terror? Now, the sisters enjoy hugging each other. Their fear has vanished, and they can express their love for each other much more easily.

Evidence supporting the process of reincarnation is strong. I personally find the accounts that I've researched compelling and fascinating, and my own experiences have cemented the belief firmly in my mind. Furthermore, in communicating with Spirit as a medium, I've been told many times by different energies about the reincarnation process. With all of these things in mind, I offer you these related questions and answers to contemplate.

What is a life contract? How does it affect the life we're living?

Many metaphysicians, from Theosophy founder Helena P. Blavatsky to current popular medium Sylvia Browne, believe that before we enter into a physical incarnation, we plot a life contract or chart that maps out the important events we wish to undertake in our upcoming lifetime. We do this in the spirit world with the help of our guides, teachers, and loved ones. These charts also reflect the important life lessons and karmic issues we choose to work through in our incarnation. This contract includes all of the other souls that play a part in our work, family, romantic, and social interactions.

As you can imagine, completing this chart before we incarnate is a huge undertaking. The contract, however, helps us to stay focused on our life lessons, the main reasons for undergoing a physical incarnation. Although we can learn a great deal and progress spiritually as a soul of pure energy on the Other Side, obstacles, setbacks, and frustrations help us to grow faster and more fully—and there aren't many of these in the afterlife. Only physical incarnations, where we must grapple with many difficulties, can truly teach us how to overcome them while keeping a loving, spiritual perspective. This is the reason many souls choose to reincarnate after having lived physical lifetimes in the past.

So reincarnation is a choice?

Like almost everything on the Other Side, the decision to reincarnate or to stay in the energy state in the afterlife lies completely with each individual soul. Our spirit guides and teachers may help us to see the benefits of a possible incarnation spent working on certain life lessons, karmic issues, and goals, but only the individual can make the actual choice to reincarnate. There is no pressure either way.

How long does it take for someone to reincarnate?

The answer to this question varies from soul to soul. My metaphysical instructors proposed that most individuals choose to stay in the planes of the afterlife until most of the people in their particular soul group (usually members of their immediate family and close friends) have transitioned out of the physical body. For many, this takes approximately sixty years, if you're measuring time according to Earth's reality. However, scientific studies of reincarnation like the ones cited above highlight instances of souls returning in new physical bodies within families, and it's these family members that recognize the new person as the reincarnation of a deceased relative.

For example, Dr. Jim Tucker (whom I mentioned previously) recounts the story of a boy named William who seemed without a doubt to be the reincarnation of his grandfather John. This child had congenital heart defects that corresponded to the fatal gunshot wounds that John suffered as a police officer. William also mentioned to his mother, John's daughter, several pieces of information about his life as John that William could not have possibly known, especially at the young age he was when he recounted them. So although souls may wait on the Other Side to reunite with their loved ones after they make their transitions, they may also choose to reincarnate within their family group again, especially if they have lessons that can only be learned with those particular souls.

Can you explain more about soul groups? Have we lived with all of the people we know in previous lives?

Reincarnation with familiar souls seems to occur quite often. This can be attributed to the phenomenon of soul groups, particular bands of souls that are attached to each other through love and karmic ties. Have you ever met a stranger and instantly felt a strong connection to him? This is one way to recognize a member of your unique soul group. For instance, I have a husband and two sons in this lifetime. In past-life regression experiences, I have recognized both of my sons and my husband, although they have not appeared together in the scenes from those lifetimes that I've witnessed. This doesn't necessarily mean that they weren't present; I may have only seen flashes of moments from those lives that only included that one other particular soul.

It's also important to note that just because I'm a woman and mother in this lifetime, my gender may have been different in other lives, and my sons may not have lived as my children. In one past-life regression I recently experienced, I saw myself as a woman in Palestine in 204 A.D., and I recognized my husband in that lifetime as my older son's soul. I know I've been a male soldier and a pirate in other past lives, although I don't recall seeing any members of my immediate family in those experiences. This doesn't mean that they weren't there, but those particular souls could have chosen to stay on the Other Side for a time while I incarnated once again. Perhaps a lesson in one of those lifetimes was learning to get along without them. I don't know. The point here is that many times, close friends and family members will turn up in our past-life memories because we make an agreement with them as part of our life contract to incarnate with us so we can work through karmic issues and lessons that we've undertaken.

It's hard to say whether or not you've lived in previous incarnations with every single person in your present life. Folks who assume special roles in your life—like your siblings, parents, spouse, children, and other close relatives and friends—have often lived at least once with you. If you're interested in reincarnation, you might consider experiencing a past-life regression so that you can pinpoint different people in your life that you recognize in a past incarnation and consider what spiritual lessons the two of you may be working on together in this lifetime. We often incarnate to balance karma with other souls through the challenges we face here on the earth plane.

So it's possible that my son could be the same soul as my father, who passed away when I was a teenager?

Yes, it's definitely possible. It's also possible that the soul that was your father will wait in the afterlife until you and all of his other close loved ones make the transition to that plane of existence. This way, he can welcome you, enjoy seeing you again, and you can all compare your life experiences to judge whether you've completed what you set out to do and to examine how well you've balanced your karma.

From the research I've investigated, it appears that children who are reincarnations of recognizable family members often begin speaking about their experiences at a very young age. The boy Dr. Tucker mentioned, William, started talking at the age of three about his life as his grandfather John. Some children may not speak of being a specific family member, but they'll still recall their lifetimes, especially the most recent one. One of my church members, Michelle, told me about her young daughter, Sam, suddenly declaring one day in the supermarket that her daddy had shot her. When Michelle, embarrassed by this announcement in a public place, told Sam that her father loved her and would never hurt her, Sam replied, "No, my other daddy." She also showed her mother where she'd been shot. Michelle was appalled, having raised her daughter in a peaceful household where she wouldn't be exposed to violence, and she couldn't figure out where Sam had gotten such a notion. At the time, Michelle didn't know anything about past lives, and she wishes now that she'd been able to ask more questions that might have revealed more about Sam's previous incarnation.

If you believe your child may be the reincarnation of a passed loved one, try asking some questions like, "So where were you before you came here?" or "What was your life like before you lived with Mommy and Daddy?" I tried this with my boys when they were very small, but both of them looked at me like I had three heads. (Those are practical, earth-based Capricorns for you, even at three years old!) This reaction led me to believe my boys have no memories of their previous lives, at least not at the forefront of their thoughts. They could easily access these incarnations, though, if they wish, just like the rest of us can.

My first pregnancy ended in a miscarriage. Is my newborn daughter the same soul as that original baby?

Again, this is one possible scenario. Miscarried and aborted souls do possess consciousness; I've had many of these spirits come through in mediumship messages to talk about their circumstances, usually stunning the people who are sitting for the readings. Realize, however, that there is no pain involved for them as their journey to the earth plane comes to an end. They simply return to pure energy, and they may choose to come back into a body at another time. Because they've already mapped out a life chart with certain lessons and agreements made with members of their soul groups, they may come into another body within that family, which would be the case in this question. They may rewrite parts of their chart regarding the relationships that they'd originally planned and still incarnate within the soul group, but with other members who can also help them to learn their lessons. Again, it's up to that individual soul what is chosen.

It should be noted, however, that miscarriages and abortions can be written into a soul's life plan in order for specific individuals to learn certain lessons. For instance, a mother soul may write a miscarriage into her life chart so that she can experience pain and grief at an intimate level. The soul that agrees to be miscarried may not plan out an entire lifetime but simply accepts this role to help the mother soul. Abortions may be written in with the understanding that the mother soul may choose a different path by exercising her free will, thus allowing the child soul to be born and to follow his or her life chart. The lessons learned through either choice are important ones for the mother soul, and these types of larger spiritual lessons truly exemplify how deeply souls love each other in agreeing to be parts of these experiences.

Do animals reincarnate? Do they ever come back as human beings?

Most metaphysicians agree that many animals do reincarnate, coming back to a physical existence as another animal. Pets, especially dogs and cats, seem to do this fairly often, and it may be to join the human counterparts they remember from previous incarnations. I've had animals in readings show me what they're doing on the Other Side, however, so not all pets reincarnate, or they may not do so immediately after making their transition.

Some people believe that animals do eventually reincarnate as human beings. This doctrine is prevalent in Hinduism and may hinge on either karma or the natural progression of the soul. In my work as a medium and my research into past-life regressions, I've never encountered a human soul that has spoken of a previous incarnation as an animal. I'm not ruling this out, because I don't possess every answer as to how the Universe works, but just like you, I can only base my beliefs on my own experiences.

How can I tell how many past lives I've had?

Many people have literally lived hundreds of lives, so finding out about each and every incarnation you've had could probably take you an entire lifetime by itself! If you're interested in researching your own past lives, read the materials referenced in this book and any others you can find that may help you to understand reincarnation better. You may also wish to purchase a CD or guided-imagery tape that takes you through your own past-life regression experience, or you may want to schedule an appointment with a regressionist (someone trained to facilitate past-life regressions) so that you can access one of your past lives.

It's been my experience that we recall the lifetimes that may be having an impact on our current incarnation. For instance, if you're experiencing chronic pain in this lifetime, setting the intention to get to the cause of that problem will help you to investigate a life that may be at the root of that pain. I mentioned earlier that I was a pirate in one lifetime. In accessing memories of that life, I discovered that my job was to dispatch, quickly and efficiently, the prisoners of the ships we invaded. I observed bedraggled sailors begging for their lives, and I saw myself swinging my cutlass dispassionately, cutting off their cries with swift and deadly strokes. I realized from that experience that part of the chronic pain I have in my right shoulder stems from that past lifetime. My soul is still trying to balance the karma of that incarnation, and I carry a great deal of remorse and guilt over my actions. This manifests as pain in my shoulder and as an intolerance for whining (my children can attest to this, I'm sure).

When I learned this was part of the cause of my shoulder issues, I worked on releasing my feelings of guilt and shame from that lifetime. I still have some shoulder problems, but I believe I helped my soul progression by trying to forgive myself for those bloody actions so many years ago. You, too, may discover a connection to a chronic injury or emotional issue that stems from a past-life experience.

~

As with any controversial subject, reincarnation needs more investigation to be proven as a fact in the minds of many philosophers, thinkers, and spiritual seekers. However, research continues to accumulate supporting its reality. And like everything else in this book, you personally need to research the subject to see if it fits with your belief system. I believe that acquiring knowledge in this lifetime (or our many lifetimes) is one of the primary goals we possess. The argument that living many lives and enduring myriad experiences enhances us as intelligent spiritual beings is compelling. Perhaps in your own search, you'll discover fascinating details and come to some exciting and important conclusions about yourself. You'll never know until you start looking.

NEGATIVE ENERGY

Inevitably, when folks discover that I'm a medium, a common question arises: aren't you scared? From my perspective, I might consider asking a window washer the same question (remember how I said I'm afraid of heights?). I would assume, though, that Mr. Window Washer has learned how to negotiate the cables to stay safe while doing his job, thus classifying him as a competent professional. I believe I've done the same in my work, and that a lot of the fear and negativity that attaches itself to mediumship is actually the stuff of fiction, film, and fantasy.

In our Western culture, the media, especially Hollywood, has conditioned us to believe that spirit contact is evil, wrong, and scary. Looking back, I can think of several movies I grew up watching where ghosts and spirits were malevolent and downright dangerous: *The Exorcist. The Shining. The Amityville*

Horror (yes, I realize this was based on a nonfiction book—I read that, too, and it scared the pants off me). *Poltergeist. The Haunting.* I'm sure you can think of a few others, too, in which the characters in the film are terrorized and sometimes killed by sinister spirits bent on wreaking havoc. These violent images leave indelible impressions on all of us, especially when we're young and vulnerable and we're still shaping a world view.

If we add to this warped perspective fundamental or narrow religious convictions, belief in a negative supernatural world becomes entrenched in our minds. As mentioned in the chapter "Religion and Spirit," many denominations have declared spirit contact off-limits to their followers, promising dire consequences if this edict is ignored. One way to convince people to follow your orders is to threaten their safety if they stray, and this is exactly what many religions do to keep their devotees in line. By feeding the fear that spirit contact is evil, the energy surrounding the practice becomes more and more negative because of these attitudes that people hold.

Never underestimate the great power that the mind has to induce states of panic and fear, which is just what some mainstream religions want. If they can hold on to their members by scaring them, they will. History shows us too many examples of a fearful mindset overtaking a population of seemingly rational people, usually instigated by some zealous institution: The Salem witchcraft trials. The Inquisition. Nazi Germany. The McCarthy era in American politics. These sobering reminders caution us not to be too quick to jump on the proverbial bandwagon.

So, through our manipulation by the entertainment industry and some religious institutions, we fear spirit contact as something evil and threatening. And, just like a child who is told not to stand on the chair to reach the off-limits cookie jar, we find ourselves dragging our own stool over to the shelf, fascinated by that which is forbidden. What to do?

First, we need to acknowledge that many things that aren't completely understood can also be frightening. Don't you think Neil Armstrong was scared before taking his first steps on the moon? He'd been trained as an astronaut, but no one had walked on another heavenly body before. In the same vein, none of us fully comprehend spirit contact and how it works, but that doesn't mean we shouldn't explore the possibilities. We minimize the unknown as much as possible, and we trust in our abilities before we strike out on our own, just as Neil Armstrong did.

We also need to recognize that the movie industry is a business, and it's out to entertain the public. What's going to sell more tickets: an action-packed thrill ride in which a ghost chases people and causes peril, or a gentle film where all a spirit does is talk to his loved ones? Box-office receipts point to the first one, not the second, so what's Hollywood going to continue to produce? We have to acknowledge that sometimes we enjoy it when someone scares us. Hollywood and Stephen King probably know this better than anybody. We can't allow fiction to color our thoughts and our belief in positive spirit connections.

We've already talked about the bias concerning spirit communication because of scripture references, so I won't rehash those here. What I will say is this: it's much more important to cultivate a personal relationship with God that highlights your inherent divinity. If you truly believe you're a divine being, then all fear melts away. This has nothing to do with ego or a sense of self-importance. It has everything to do with recognizing that if we are all divine, nothing can hurt us in any way unless we allow it to do so.

This attitude can be applied to all areas of our lives, not just to spirit communication. First Lady Eleanor Roosevelt wrote in her memoir, "No one can make you feel inferior without your consent." Again, if we can take this quotation to heart and examine it devoid of ego, we understand that, as divine beings, we're perfect and whole as God created us. Nothing can harm us. It is with this conviction and attitude that spirit contact should be approached. It is, after all, another gift from Creator, and when we treat it with respect, and we honor our spirit communicators and ourselves, we achieve awesome rewards.

With these things in mind, let's look at some questions concerning negative energy.

Do I have to do anything to protect myself from Spirit?

The use of the word *from* in this question concerns me, because it makes Spirit sound like a band of marauders out to get you! Again, if you really believe this, then you're going to attract lower-energy vibrations if you try to work between the worlds as a medium. Yes, lower-energy vibrations do exist, just as higher vibration energies do. The key is in the Natural Law of Attraction, which states that like attracts like. If you can keep your own vibrational energy high by maintaining a loving, positive attitude about yourself and your world, then you'll only attract into your energy field positive and loving energies, whether they're inhabitants of this plane or other planes of existence.

I stress to all of my mediumship students the use of a centering meditation at the beginning of each day to set up a positive energy field around the body, so only beneficial energies are attracted. I do this meditation every morning, and I encourage everyone to do something similar, whether you want to be a spirit medium or not. In this meditation, you surround yourself with Divine White Light, the energy that is Creator, and you affirm for yourself that as you dwell within this Light, only positive and loving energies can reach you. If you'd like to incorporate this simple meditation into your daily routine, go to the appendix of this book to learn how.

Affirmations can also be very helpful in changing a negative mindset. By repeating positive statements about yourself, your energy, and your ability to attract good, you change the actual vibration that you carry, thus naturally attracting into your auric field more and more beneficial thoughts, feelings, events, and spirit communications. Try saying aloud some of the following affirmations during your day:

"I am a positive magnet attracting loving, helpful spirit energies."

"I am a divine being, perfect in every way."

"I am a positive and clear channel for spirit communication."

"I am constantly surrounded by the loving energy of God/Creator/Source."

"I am surrounded by helpful, loving, positive spirit friends who want only the best for me."

If you can keep your mind in a high, positive place, you'll only attract good into your world. And if you believe you're connected to Creator through your own inner divinity, nothing can dwell in that beneficent vibration except equally high energies.

What are poltergeists?

This term comes from German roots, indicating a noisy spirit that is usually disruptive. Activity is usually characterized by noises with unknown origins, including knocking and tapping, disturbances of stationary objects, slamming doors, flickering lights, and other similar phenomena. Most paranormal researchers agree, however, that in most cases, these occurrences are not attributable to ghost activity. Instead, they can usually be tied to an adolescent in close proximity to the disturbances. Known as the "human agent," these teenagers, usually girls, unconsciously cause the disruptions through psychokinesis (PK), the ability to manipulate things using the energy of the brain.

The phenomena usually occur around the onset of puberty, when an adolescent is caught in the throes of emotional, mental, and sexual confusion or turmoil. The teen will usually have no idea that she's causing the problem, but professional help sought through a counselor or mental health practitioner can help ease the outbursts of PK activity. Usually, over time, the disturbances diminish as the teen becomes more comfortable in her changing body and new role as a young adult. So, most alleged poltergeist activity, though certainly paranormal, doesn't truly fit in with any discussion of spirit contact.

There are isolated incidents of hauntings and ghost activity that may be poltergeists at work, but these seem to be few and far between and, naturally, hard to quantify by paranormal investigators. Again, in my opinion, one has to assess the energy of the place where the activity is noticed and work to change the vibration to a more positive, loving one. If this change is achieved, a lower-vibration entity simply cannot stay attached to it because the Natural Law of Attraction, one of the immutable Laws governing the way the Universe works, would not allow this to happen.

Are exorcisms real? Can people truly be possessed by demons?

To answer this question, we must once again examine the influence that religious convictions hold for some people. A belief in demonic energies controlled by Satan is prevalent in many fundamental Christian denominations, especially those that understand the Bible as unequivocal, literal truth. The New Testament highlights several instances of Jesus exorcising demons from unfortunate souls; therefore, those who read the Bible literally would have a hard time disputing the fact that Jesus drove out these evil spirits, thus curing the afflicted. Many modern thinkers, however, believe that the people Jesus healed in these instances were most likely suffering from mental health disorders like schizophrenia or physical issues like epilepsy.

In the early days of Christianity, when the belief that Satan and his minions were real and viable threats, many mentally disturbed individuals were thought to be possessed. As this belief gained in popularity, more and more physical and emotional issues were attributed to the evil work of demons. It makes sense that the writers of the New Testament, who recorded the stories of Jesus centuries after his death, included this popular notion in their accounts. Today, more expansive Christian denominations agree that troubled people will get more help from psychiatrists, psychologists, and therapists than from exorcists.

In my own experiences as a minister, healer, and counselor, I've met individuals who are completely convinced that negative energies are attached to them. I've listened to accounts of people describing terrible and frightening encounters with unseen forces that have injured them physically and tormented them mentally. I've never seen any physical evidence to support these claims, however, and what I've seen clairvoyantly about these folks has indicated nothing to me but someone desperately in need of psychiatric help. I don't want to sound cold or dispassionate about any of this, because mental illness is a very real, very scary, and very dangerous affliction. I know; someone very close to me suffers from a mental disorder. However, I cannot in all good conscience condone the idea of exorcisms and demon possession, because in all of my work over the years, I've never seen it. And I don't believe I ever will if I continue to work in the loving Light of Divine Creator.

**I feel surrounded by negativity. I don't know if they're spirits
or just my imagination, but what can I do to change the energy?**

If you've read this far, you've surmised by now that I'm a big
believer in the Law of Attraction. If you feel that negativity surrounds you, it may be because your own energy vibration is low. To heighten it, try the White Light meditation in
the appendix of this book and practice it on a regular basis.
Incorporate some of the above affirmations into your daily
routine; say them aloud when you're driving the car, washing
the dishes, or weeding the garden. Altering your mindset and
releasing negative thought patterns are integral to heightening your own energy vibration.

Clean your house, your workspace, and anywhere else you
spend a significant amount of time. Just like dust, energy becomes trapped in cluttered areas, thus attracting more low
energy. Do some energetic "spring cleaning" and throw away
items that are broken or useless. Donate old clothes, appliances, or items to a local charity organization. Once you've rid
yourself of unnecessary junk, spend time vacuuming, dusting, scrubbing, and polishing. As you clean, visualize heavy or
dark energy leaving the space, replacing it in your mind with
fresh, uplifting, positive light energy. To go one step further,
consider incorporating feng shui, the Eastern art of furniture
placement and space arrangement, which encourages positive
energy to flow more easily in a home or office. Many good
books and websites include tips on how to enhance the energy in your space by utilizing these techniques.

Consider, too, how you're feeling physically. When we're
worn out, stressed, or in pain, our energy level drops, and our

auric field often becomes muddy and dark. This is another way we can attract lower vibrations without knowing it. If you can afford some special treatments, like a body massage, reflexology, or a session with a qualified energy healer, book an appointment for yourself. If not, make time to take a hot shower or bath, listen to quiet music, or read a book of inspirational stories. Exercise regularly, which releases endorphins into the bloodstream, giving your body a natural pick-me-up. Eat healthy foods and partake of natural beverages. All of these activities help you to feel better, which will drive your energy higher and help you to attract more positive vibrations into your field.

Never believe anyone who tells you that a curse has been placed on you and that she can lift it from you for a fee. This is a scam, and you should run screaming in the opposite direction from anyone who tries to con you this way. If you believe you're cursed, you're buying into the entire mindset that someone else can negatively affect you, which denies your personal power and responsibility. The only person that can control your actions and the events of your life is you. Yes, others can send you negative energy, usually prompted by envy or dislike. You, however, do not have to accept any energy that is sent to you. Stay wrapped in the Divine Light that is your birthright as a child of God, and nothing like this can hurt you.

Finally, please revisit your connection to Creator. Prayer and meditation bring harmony and balance to many because, when we feel loved, accepted, and connected to this Higher Power, we feel at peace with everything around us. If prayer is difficult for you, think of it instead as talking to God, just like you'd speak to an old friend. That's really what Creator is, anyway.

As you can hopefully surmise by now, negative energy is something that can be controlled and managed, and a great deal of how you do this depends on your personal mindset and belief system. If you keep your energy vibration in a high, loving, positive place, you'll experience very little negative energy in working with Spirit. If you keep the Divine Source at the forefront of all of your intentions in connecting with Spirit, you won't have to worry about lower entities somehow sneaking in to trick you or bother you. Remember that spirit communication is a natural skill, like dancing, and you can shape the dance you wish to experience by wisely choosing partners, learning the right steps, and practicing your routines. Know that Creator will bless you with good energy if you ask for it, and you will never have anything to fear.

WHO, ME?
A MEDIUM?

When I first began studying mediumship in 1996, the world was a different place. I'd met a few other folks who were interested in spirit communication, but I had to go to Indiana, a whole state away and the home of a Spiritualist camp, to receive any formal training in mediumship development. The Internet may have been around, but I didn't know anything about it, let alone maintain relationships with other potential mediums via websites or chatrooms. My world was much, much smaller, and those of us who were focusing on our relationships with Spirit seemed isolated and alone.

As I write this in 2009, that segregated and sometimes lonely existence seems a long way away. Nowadays, mediums appear to be everywhere: on hundreds of websites all over cyberspace; on television programs where celebrity mediums give readings to members of their studio audiences; on reality shows focusing on living a "normal" life as a spirit communicator; even in dramatic TV programs, movies, and novels as protagonists and heroes struggling through their work with the dead.

Why such a pronounced upsurge in this attention? I think it has to do with the fact that more and more everyday people are beginning to see mediumship and spirit communication as something acceptable and normal. They may even be recognizing a great truth about this work, something that fills me with hope and joy whenever I consider it:

We are *all* mediums. We can *all* communicate with Spirit. We just need to learn how to do it.

Just like intuition, the ability to connect with those in Spirit is a natural talent latent in us all. Some of us recognize and utilize this ability with more ease and panache than others, but it's present in everyone. What separates an "everyday" medium from a professional one is the amount of time and effort put into the study of developing those connection skills. And that, of course, is a free-will decision.

In my first book, *So You Want to Be a Medium?*, I explained how mediumship is accessible to everyone, which scientific principles and Natural Laws affect it, and I outlined a step-by-step process for readers to follow to help them begin to open the door to the spirit world. If you're interested in studying mediumship, I suggest you take a look at that book. In this chapter, however, we'll highlight a few questions I'm asked on a regular basis concerning individual spirit contact and the process that makes it a reality.

Can I learn to become a medium, even if I don't feel I was born with any special extrasensory perception?

Whether you think it's present or not, you *were* born with inherent intuitive capabilities. The key to psychic and mediumship work is learning how you receive your messages and how to interpret them when they come through.

When we use the term *clairvoyant* (clear-seeing), we're literally describing one way a person may receive a psychic or spirit message. He may either see a vision of something in his mind, or, in rarer cases, he may actually see a spirit entity with his physical eyes. A *clairaudient* person hears messages either through his physical ears or in his mind. A *clairsentient* perceives messages as feelings or impressions, sometimes in different places in his body. *Claircognizance* is a knowing that comes to a person as a clear and definite thought in the mind. All of these senses correspond to physical ones that we use every day. When we learn to recognize our "clairs" and pay attention to the sensations, impressions, thoughts, and visions that we receive in these ways, we're moving forward in our development as psychics and mediums.

Why is meditation so important in spirit communication work?

Meditation teaches your mind to be focused and disciplined, which serves you well once you open yourself up to the spirit world with the purpose of receiving messages. It also teaches you how to set an intention in your work with Spirit, which is vitally important. Success follows when a firm intention is set and combined with hard work. Meditation is the best way to have an active relationship with your spirit guides, teachers, and angels, who can then interact usefully in your life as helpers and coaches. Finally, meditation helps its practitioners keep a more loving, peaceful state of mind, which in turn attracts more positive energies in both the physical and spiritual worlds.

But I can't meditate! Does this mean I'll never be able to communicate with Spirit?

Remember that saying you can't do something is energetic suicide to success! Please cancel that negative thought and begin programming your mind to believe that it can achieve a meditative state. Repeat an affirmation like, "I easily reach a meditative state where all of my intentions are successfully realized." Just changing your attitude will enable you to approach meditation from a better perspective.

Perhaps you've tried meditation a few times and don't feel as if you've attained success. Perhaps the whole idea of it intimidates you, as it does many. Maybe you can't seem to find the time to incorporate it into your day. Let's take these issues one at a time.

If you've attempted meditation in the past but feel it went badly, try changing the time, location, or type of meditation. Don't meditate in the evening if you're already tired and might fall asleep, and make sure you sit up for your meditation instead of lying down. Clear your meditation space of all distractions, including the telephone, pets, or children. Play relaxing music if it appeals to you. Take the time to set up a space that's comfortable and appealing, a place where you want to spend time. All of these factors can contribute to a successful meditation experience.

Only attempt a very short meditation at the beginning of your study, which will help you to focus completely and will set a reasonable, attainable goal. (It's also much easier to fit a short meditation into a busy life schedule.) Try five minutes at first, and concentrate on clearing your mind of all thought as you focus on your breathing. This may not seem like much, but your brain must learn to settle by releasing unnecessary thoughts. Anytime a thought such as "Did I run the dishwasher?" or "I hope my dad remembers his doctor's appointment tomorrow" comes into your mind, simply release it and bring your focus back to your breathing and the void in between thoughts. Five minutes is actually a long time to continuously bring back your focus, especially when you're new to meditation. Once you've mastered this, you can try a ten-minute meditation to further instruct your logical brain to allow empty space in your mind. It's this space that will someday fill with spirit communications.

Another good meditation to master is one that hones your concentration abilities. Choose a word like *peace*, *love*, or even *focus*, and hold this word in your mind for five minutes. Whenever stray thoughts wander in, simply let them go and bring your focus back to your word. You can use a focus picture in your mind instead of a word, too, as a variation, or if you feel you're a more visual person. This meditation exercise trains your mind to stop shooting random thoughts at you every waking moment.

You can also try a guided meditation experience. Metaphysical stores and suppliers offer many choices in guided meditation CDs or tapes, which can help you more easily connect with the spirit world. You can also use the meditation scripts included in the appendix of this book; read them into a recording device and then listen to them on headphones to facilitate a relaxing, Spirit-oriented meditation. You could also sign up for a meditation class at a local health spa or metaphysical shop that will teach you different techniques.

Don't give up. Many people try meditation for a few days, become frustrated, and abandon the practice. If you're serious about spirit connections, you have to be serious about meditation. Like everything worthwhile, meditation, and, in turn, spirit work, takes practice and dedication. You *can* meditate, and eventually you'll find yourself longing for the time spent in quiet, serene contemplation.

What if I'm not communicating with an angel or guide, but with Satan or a demon? How can I tell the difference?

Please be sure to read the chapter in this book entitled "Negative Energy," where I discuss beliefs and attitudes about this subject. These shape your intention, which needs to be pure and positive when you approach spirit work. If you believe you're going to contact something negative, this is exactly what the Natural Law of Attraction will bring to you! If, however, you set your intention that you're a perfect and divine channel for spirit communication, then you will be, and only higher-vibration spirits will come through in your work.

Discernment, or the ability to tell spirits apart from each other, is a skill every medium must develop, and it can be challenging. Since many mediums are clairsentient and feel when a spirit comes in, they need to develop techniques to be able to tell vibrations apart. The differences in vibrational energies can be quite subtle, but if time is spent paying close attention to how certain guides, teachers, and angels feel when they present themselves, a medium can learn to differentiate between energies. It's also important for a medium to be in charge of how energies present themselves so that she can tell who's who in the spirit world. Some of these techniques are discussed in my book *So You Want to Be a Medium?* Please refer to that book for more guidance.

One key way to tell if a spirit has your best interests at heart is from the message delivered. It's been my experience that spirit teachers will offer guidance, but they will never tell you unequivocally what to do. They understand that this is interfering in your free will, and they won't cross that line. If a spirit you're working with insists that you must do a certain thing, you need to question this, especially when the advice may be dangerous or put you in some sort of jeopardy. If you ever feel the slightest bit negative or unsettled by advice given from Spirit, don't take it and end the communication. It might be that you tapped into a lower-energy vibration. Go back, reset your intention, and ask again. This should clear away any doubt, fear, or negativity.

How do I know if the messages I receive are accurate or true?

The best way to determine this is to keep a written record of your interactions with Spirit. When you meditate to connect with your guides, or you ask for spirit help with a certain situation, record the date in a notebook, along with what you communicated and any other experiences you had. If you asked for guidance and you saw a blob of yellow in your meditation, write it down. Most people miss the guidance they've received from Spirit because they think it's meaningless or unimportant. That blob of yellow that your spirit teacher sent to you represents something—a feeling, a course of action, a thought—and it's your job as the medium to figure out what it means. Colors have very specific associations in symbology. Do some research to find out what yellow may mean as a color correspondence. Or simply rely on your own instincts and interpretations. How do you feel when you see that particular shade of yellow? Does it make you happy? Perhaps your guide is trying to show you that a certain choice in the matter will bring you joy. Everything that you receive in a communication is relevant, which is why writing down your impressions is important. You can then go back over them and puzzle out the meanings.

Once you understand the message that Spirit sent to you, you can then check its accuracy, especially if it's something predictive in nature. For instance, let's pretend you asked if you'd receive good weather for your golf game on Thursday. Your spirit guide showed you the color blue, which you wrote down in your notebook, interpreting this to symbolize clear skies for your round. On Thursday, you play golf under a brilliant azure sky, and when you return home, you record in your notebook that the blue color and your interpretation were accurate. Give your spirit guide a cookie for sending you the correct information, and be proud of yourself for your insight.

However, let's say your guide sent you the color blue, and it poured rain the entire time you golfed. Miserable and cold, you returned home, upset that Spirit sent you the wrong information. Well, did your spirit guide give you the wrong answer, or did you just misinterpret it? Maybe your guide sent the color blue to you because water looks blue, and he was trying to tell you it was going to rain a river! In this case, you should record in your notebook what happened, and then make another note that the color blue doesn't equate to clear skies but rather to rain. You can also talk out loud to your spirit guide as you do this, so that he understands that you're unhappy because of the snafu in the communication process. Tell him that you'd like to see actual *rain showers* if you ask a similar question in the future, or tell him that you'd like the color blue to symbolize a clear sky. This is the best way to avoid communication problems in the future.

Yes, it takes a while sometimes, especially since once you establish a method of communication, you should ask for a weather update from Spirit every day so predictions can be made and checked. There's nothing wrong with expecting your communications with Spirit to be accurate. Sometimes, though, you're going to misinterpret something, and you need to explain to your guides how you think you all can work better together and develop strategies and symbolism that will enhance your communication.

How do you control which spirits come to you and when?

It's important always to remember the first rule of mediumship, which is *you control Spirit*. (We also talked about this rule in the chapter "Spirit Guides, Teachers, and Angels.") This means that you're in control of when you perceive spirits as opposed to when you're simply conducting the minutia of your daily life. I'm constantly amazed at folks who talk about walking around with spirit people trailing after them all day long, trying to get their attention. This is comparable to being on the telephone twenty-four hours a day, seven days a week, attempting to maintain a constant conversation. Can you see how exhausting this might be? Spirit communication is a shift in perception, and you need to learn to shift from perceiving spirits to being oblivious to them! Our spirit people want to work with us, but they certainly don't wish to drain our energy.

Even if you're a professional medium, your work with Spirit is only one part of your life. You don't have to dwell between the world of the living and the world of Spirit all the time. In fact, you shouldn't, because you chose this physical lifetime to work on more than just being a medium. Your commitment to family, friends, or other work are equally, if not more, important, which means being able to focus on balancing the checkbook, taking out the trash, solving a problem with your spouse, or playing Guitar Hero with the kids. This means scheduling time for your meditations and connections with Spirit, and, once these boundaries are set, honoring them. Your spirit people understand that you can be committed to spirit work but not available every moment of every day to focus on connections. In fact, I can almost guarantee that your spirit guides would scold you for neglecting other aspects of your life, which shape us into well-rounded individuals.

As a professional medium, I'm very committed to my work, but I'm also quite adamant about when and how I do it. It took me a long time to learn this lesson, however, and every now and then, Spirit will send me a little "test" to make sure I'm honoring myself as well as my obligations as a medium. Usually this manifests as an especially demanding client who doesn't understand why I can't perform a reading for her on my day off or why I won't spend three hours of my time trying to make a connection with her great-uncle Earl. These challenges present themselves as ways for me to reiterate my policies, or they proffer opportunities to teach someone a bit about how mediumship works. They also remind me that just because I chose a service-oriented career, it doesn't mean that I put myself and my needs last. If I'm not working, *I'm not working.* Spirit respects this when you make your intentions clear; you need to respect your needs and the demands of your earthly life, too.

When you're ready to stand between the worlds, setting a direct intention to work only in high, positive vibrations will prevent any negative spirits from getting through when you open the door to communication. If you wish to communicate with a specific spirit teacher or loved one on the Other Side, you can set this intention as well, and have every confidence that your expectation will be met. Just remember that loved ones may not be able to communicate at every moment, so they may send someone else to deliver this message, or your guides may indicate to you that contact with them isn't possible. Keep trying at a later time, hold the desire to talk to them firmly in your mind, and eventually you'll make contact.

Sometimes before I fall asleep at night, I see faces or hear voices. They don't frighten me, but I don't know what this means.

The state between wakefulness and sleep is called *hypnagogia*. Because it's similar in consciousness to meditation, the body and mind are both relaxed and open in this state. Spirits can easily access this state of mind to make impressions, which may be why you're seeing faces and hearing voices. As long as you're comfortable with this and you haven't encountered anything negative, it's fine. If you don't like it, speak to your spirit guides and ask them to only bring your loved ones or their own messages to you in your meditations. If they really want to let you know they're around or they want to bring through an important message, they'll honor your wishes and try to come through in the most clear and acceptable way.

If you're experiencing frightening energies in the hypnagogic state, do a short meditation before bed where you surround yourself with Divine White Light and hold your intention of safety and high energy firmly in your mind. Any problem vibrations should disperse.

Is using a Ouija board OK for communicating with spirits?

The Ouija board, a copyrighted name for a mass-produced device known more commonly as a talking board, was invented in the late 1800s for the purpose of communicating with those on the Other Side. By this time, Spiritualism had swept through the United States, and more and more people were interested in conducting séances and hosting spirit circles in their homes. Many spirits "rapped" out their messages, a tedious process that involved the unseen entities knocking on the walls or the séance table to express themselves. Because a certain number of raps corresponded to letters of the alphabet, this was one way for Spirit to physically communicate a message to everyone present—but, as you can imagine, a spirit session might take many long hours to produce one short, rapped message. Just like today, spiritual seekers also sought ways that they could connect with deceased loved ones without having a professional medium present.

The talking board filled this need. A smooth, wooden rectangle much like a modern gameboard with the letters of the alphabet painted on it, the talking board was held on the knees between two people seated in chairs. The sitters would then settle their fingertips lightly upon the planchette, the little triangular pointer that the spirits influenced to move. The sitters could then invite spirit entities into their home and pose questions, which would be answered by the spirits, who moved the planchette to various letters, spelling out a reply. Ouija boards, a brand name of talking board that eventually rose to prominence, are still sold in toy stores and novelty shops today. I quite vividly remember playing with one myself as a young girl.

Talking boards are legitimate ways to access the spirit realms, just as Tarot or oracle cards are legitimate means to search for the most accurate answers possible. However, talking boards are tools, just like these other objects, and they should be treated with respect. If you want to use a talking board, clear from it, before your first session, any negative energy it may hold from the manufacturing line or from those who handled it up until that point. Visualize it surrounded by Divine White Light, and ask for God's blessing upon it. Affirm aloud, "This board is blessed by Creator. It is constantly surrounded by divine loving energy, and only the highest, most appropriate, and accurate messages can channel through it."

Know that this intention will be honored, and you should be able to use your Ouija or other talking board without any problems. Whenever you set it up for use, begin your session with a prayer that only positive, loving spirit energies come through to deliver messages. This will encourage your guides, teachers, angels, and deceased loved ones to use the board as another method for communicating with you. I still advocate developing a personal relationship with your spirit people through meditation and mind-to-mind contact, but talking boards are acceptable means to use if they're treated with respect as the tools they're intended to be.

My young daughter told me she's playing with Nana in her bedroom. Her grandmother died six months ago. Is she crazy, or is she just inventing things?

Many children are very perceptive about energies manifesting around them, because no one has told them yet that it's crazy to believe in spirits and their ability to communicate. It doesn't surprise me at all that your daughter's grandmother is coming to visit her. If she were my child, I'd say something like, "How great that Grandma can still check in with you even though she's passed over to the Other Side! This must be Grandma's way of letting you know she's doing well in the afterlife. What did you talk to her about?" This way, you're encouraging your daughter to continue her connection with Grandma, and you're also letting her know that you believe in the reality of after-death communication. You're also affirming for her that mediumship is not something to be afraid of, and that this type of contact is loving and positive. Most of all, you're fostering an open and trusting relationship between you and your child, an important goal for any parent.

My son sees spirits in his bedroom when he's trying to fall asleep. This frightens and disturbs him. What can I do to help him?

First, keeping an open dialogue with your son about his experiences is very important. If you start to question the validity of what he tells you, he may stop speaking about it altogether, which really isn't healthy and can be detrimental to his mental development. Explain to him that spirits are simply energies of people who have passed away, and they like to check in with those of us on the earth plane because they miss us. If the presence of these spirits scares him, teach him to do a simple White Light meditation so that he can feel safe, protected, and in control. Remind him that he also has spirit guides, teachers, and angels that want him to feel happy, and prompt him to enlist their aid in keeping his room cleared of energies that aren't welcome. Make sure he understands that he can always firmly and definitely say to a spirit, "You are not welcome here. Leave now." As his guardian, you can also invoke other angels, like the Archangel Michael, patron of protection, to keep his bedroom cleared of lower energies.

It's most important to help him take control and to feel empowered. All children are frightened of certain things, and one of our jobs as parents is to help them overcome their fears. If you teach your child to keep his own energy loving and positive, he'll attract these same types of energies to himself, which will make all of his experiences, both with the physical world and the unseen one, better.

I really want to become a medium. What should I do?

The first thing I encourage all potential mediumship students to do is to ask, "Why do I want to do this work?" Be as honest as possible in your response. If you're interested in this work because you want to help people have a better understanding of the spirit world, or you long to bring healing to grieving folks by aiding them in connecting with their deceased loved ones, then you're in the right positive, loving energy vibration.

However, if you crave attention, power, or celebrity, you need to rethink your desire. Those answers are motivated by ego, and a medium has to learn to release the ego in order to do beneficial work. Being a medium is service-oriented, not self-oriented. Of course, you can do this work strictly for your own education and enlightenment, too, but I've found that many folks who undertake mediumship studies often become teachers to the people around them. When someone begins to work on herself as a spiritual being, others notice the positive changes, and they begin to question the seeker about the

new way she's conducting her life. Thus, a student begins to share her experiences and therefore becomes an instructor to others. When this happens (and it will), it's important to stay centered on service and not to allow your ego to take over. Keeping the mind and purpose firmly fixed on Creator and Spirit usually helps to curb our human tendency to fall into egotistical thinking and action.

Classes are a good place to start if you want to become a working medium. Because of the surge in interest in mediumship and after-death communication in the last few years, many institutions and private instructors offer workshops geared to teach seekers about the process of spirit contact. See if you can enroll by calling your local metaphysical shop and asking about possibilities, or by searching the Internet for places that offer these types of opportunities. Be sure to research a potential teacher or institution to find out how long they've been involved in metaphysical studies, what subjects they instruct, and what expectations they have of their students. If you're considering studying with a private teacher or joining her development circle, you may want to sit for a reading with her before committing. This can give you insight into the medium's approach to spirit contact, her accuracy in communicating with spirit energies, and her personality.

Be prepared to work with Spirit without a physical teacher if necessary. Some folks have a hard time finding an instructor to work with in their region, or the time commitment or financial resources conflict with their desire to study. You can still cultivate a relationship with your guides, teachers, and loved ones in Spirit if you don't have a class or circle to attend.

You may choose to gather like-minded individuals in a weekly meeting to study together, or you could simply make time to meditate every day with your guides in order to foster a closer connection to the spirit world. My first book, *So You Want to Be a Medium?*, is a step-by-step method for getting closer to the spirit world, written for any person who wishes to accomplish this. Reading that book and following the exercises outlined there may be a good way for you to start interacting with Spirit on a regular basis.

Education is the key to anything that you want to pursue. Learn as much as you can about mediumship by reading, researching, and actively engaging in it. If you're diligent and faithful, you'll achieve your goal of becoming a medium.

My friend asked me to do a reading for her. How do I prepare? What should I do in the reading?

Every psychic and/or medium is different, and all prepare to do their work in unique ways. Some need lots of quiet time, while others can jump right into a reading with little or no centering at all. In the same vein, no two readers are alike when they're working. Be sure that your friend understands that you're simply a student of mediumship, and although you're willing to try to get some messages for her, she needs to remember that you're still learning. Here are some things I advise, especially to those brand-new to messages and readings.

1. **Invite Creator into the process.** This is vital before opening the door to the spirit world, which is why i' first on the list. Connect with the God of your derstanding by asking Divine Source to be wi'

during the reading and to help you bring through the highest and the best messages possible for your friend. If you begin every communication with Spirit by connecting first to Divinity, you thus acknowledge your own divinity and the divinity of all entities that may come through from the many ethereal planes. You can then be assured that only positive and loving vibrations will touch in because only high energies can function within divine energy.

2. **Invite all of the spirit guides, angels, and loved ones that belong to your friend to be present.** These are the energies with which you want to communicate, so ask them to come forward from the spirit world so that you can recognize them and talk to them. This may seem like a no-brainer, but you'd be surprised how many students don't extend the invitation to Spirit. You also set your intention to communicate only with entities that belong to your friend by stating this aloud or firmly in your mind. Once you've put out the invitation, take a moment to close your eyes and sense Spirit gathering around you.

3. **Start talking, and stay out of your left brain as much as you can.** Our brains are divided into two sections: the left brain, which controls rational thought, and the right brain, which controls imagination and intuition. When we're working with Spirit, we need to stay in our right brain as much as possible, because we need to allow the flow of information from Spirit to come unhindered and without judgment. The left brain is great

for doing the taxes and setting the DVR to record a TV show, but it also criticizes and analyzes everything that the creative and intuitive right brain offers. In a reading with Spirit, the object is to bring through the messages that need to be heard, and the only way to do this is to allow the right brain to do its job. This is another reason why meditation is so important to functioning well as a medium; meditation teaches the left brain to remain silent while the right brain is working. In your reading for your friend, try to allow the information you receive to flow through you, as if you're a pipe or a channel, and don't analyze what you're receiving. This is difficult when you sense something that your left brain criticizes as silly or insignificant, so don't allow your left brain to interfere! The medium's job in a reading is to relay what Spirit communicates. It's up to your friend to figure out what the message means.

4. **If your friend says no to a piece of information you receive, it's not the end of the world.** We all get things wrong sometimes. It may be that you've misunderstood what Spirit is trying to communicate. You're allowed—you're human, right? It's also possible that your friend just doesn't understand the information that you've delivered. She may not recognize someone who comes in from Spirit because he died before she was born. If she goes back to other family members and checks, though, she may very well find that particular great-uncle or distant cousin. She may not understand a predictive piece of information about her career or her relation-

ship because it hasn't happened yet. When this happens to me (and yes, it happens to professional readers, too), I ask my client to write the information down or remember that we talked about it, because it may make more sense when she's had time to think about it or to ask family about it. Don't give up if someone says no—just keep going.

5. **Remember that touching in with Spirit should be fun and rewarding, not gloomy or troubling.** If you or your friend are not enjoying the process, please do yourselves a favor and stop. Spirit communication is a method for spreading love throughout the Universe, from the other planes to us here in the physical world. If you're irritated, frustrated, bored, or angry about the process, there's no reason to continue. If your friend becomes upset or sad, it's all right for her to end the messages. Let go of your judgment about yourself— that this means you're a terrible medium, or that you're a failure—and allow what needs to happen to unfold. Maybe you just need more practice with your guides and with your meditations on your own before you try to work with other energies. Perhaps your friend is still hurting after saying goodbye to a recently departed loved one, or can't handle the crises she's having in her life. Whatever the case, thank your guides and Creator for helping you, and be OK with whatever has happened. You learned something from the experience, and contemplating it in your own time should

prove to be valuable to your progression as a medium and as a person.

⁓

Spirit is available to every one of us, every moment of every day, if we can put our faith in the reality of communication. Yes, you *are* a medium, because we've all been given the ability to speak to Spirit and to understand the responses that we receive. Whether you decide to pursue mediumship studies is, of course, completely up to you. Knowing, however, that you always have access to a wonderful team of spirit helpers can bring comfort and upliftment in trying times. Although a lifetime on the physical plane may be challenging, we're meant to find happiness and joy in our existence. Spirit can help us to achieve this, if we can make room for that aid in our lives.

SPIRIT ODDS AND ENDS

In my kitchen, we have a junk drawer. It's the niche where miscellaneous objects end up: scissors, tape, stray batteries, eraserless pencil stumps, ticket stubs, miniature flashlights. It's not that this detritus of the mundane isn't important— God knows I'd never find the calculator or the plumber's business card if it weren't for the junk drawer. It's just that it's the stuff that doesn't have a place anywhere else.

Some questions are like that. I'd like to file them in a specific category in this book, but they just don't seem to fit. They're still important questions, though, ones that are asked time and time again by inquisitive folks. Therefore, we'll call them Spirit odds and ends.

By the way . . . while you're rummaging around in there, can you hand me the glue stick?

I went to a psychic for a reading, and she told me my husband is not my soul mate. What should I do?

I think the most important thing to consider here is why you feel a psychic needs to evaluate the strength or depth of your relationship with your husband. *You are in control of your life, no matter what a psychic or medium tells you.* If you went to a reading to gauge the energy of your personal relationship, that's fine, but it's ridiculous to get upset or agitated if a reader tells you something like this. Do you love your husband? Do you want to stay married to him? Only you can answer these questions, and only you can decide how you wish to act based on your feelings. A reading gives you an idea of the energies that are currently around you in many aspects of your life, and it can predict what circumstances may come to pass if you continue to generate the same type of energy. You can always exercise your free will and change the events and the outcome in any situation.

This question also implies a belief in the popular notion of soul mates, a topic that is debated in metaphysics. As mentioned earlier, I do believe we incarnate in soul groups, where we interact with souls we recognize for the purpose of working on lessons we agreed upon together. The notion of a soul mate suggests that there is only one individual spirit energy with whom our soul is perfectly matched. Although this is an appealing idea because of its sheer romance, the truth is that we probably wouldn't learn very much pertaining to the evolution of our spirit if we continuously faced every challenge in every lifetime with the same exact soul. It makes more sense to me that we need to interact with many different souls in innumerable unique experiences so that we can learn as much as possible. And, if you think about it, there are probably several people in your life right now that might fit the category of "soul mate"—someone to whom you feel an intense and emotional bond—but is not your spouse or romantic partner. You could have this type of connection with a best friend, a child (not even your own!), a parent, or anyone else with a significant role in your life. Special people are not always romantic partners. For this reason, the soul-mate phenomenon seems unlikely to me.

I went to get a reading, but it was all about my husband. Why did this happen?

If lots of spirits showed up in your reading that belonged to your husband's family, they must have been very determined to get a message through to him. Spirit will use any means to deliver a message, and if you're related to someone that a spirit wishes to acknowledge and the spirit is persistent enough from the Other Side, chances are good that you're going to hear from him. Also: if you're married, your spouse's family becomes your family. In-laws recognize you as part of their group, so it's important to remember them when you go for a reading. My father-in-law often comes through in my readings to chat about situations in my family. I never had a chance to meet my father-in-law during my lifetime, but I feel much closer to him than I do to some of my own distant relatives because of his persistent presence from the Other Side.

If the information in your reading seemed to revolve around your husband, he may be approaching a very significant time or cycle of energy in his life. Spirit obviously saw your reading as an opportunity to address some of these issues and to highlight what your spouse needs to know about them. In any marriage, what affects one partner has a serious impact on the other and on the relationship itself. I encourage you to share the information that came through in your reading with your husband so that both of you can work on any issues together.

Many mediums have told me that they see a child spirit around me, but my wife and I have decided we don't want any more children. What does this mean?

Only your wife and you can decide what is best for your lifestyle and your family. Spirit is not trying to pressure you into anything that you don't want or can't handle. If a medium picks up on an energy around you, it's her job to tell you what she's receiving. It's your job to make sense of it. It could be that the child spirit around you is a guide for you, and you can verify this yourself by using meditations to work toward getting to know this energy to see if this is the case. The child could also be a soul that would like to be in your life, but don't feel obligated to bring that child in if your family is complete.

If that child energy is meant to be with you, he or she could manifest as a grandchild, a younger niece or nephew, a friend of one of your children, a friend's child, or in many other ways. Energies that are significant to your growth as a spiritual being will be in your life one way or the other; it's not up to you to try to control all the wheres and hows of these equations.

What is the lesson in an abortion, a miscarriage, or a stillbirth?

Only the people involved in these situations can truly figure out the exact lesson that the event helped them to learn. Because they both deal with the death of an established embryo or soul that doesn't seem to involve a conscious choice, miscarriages and stillbirths may have a variety of lessons to teach those touched by them. Perhaps the tragedy of such an event will bring certain people left behind closer together. Maybe the trauma will help someone involved to seek professional counseling, which will allow much-needed emotional, spiritual, and mental healing to take place. Physical health and well-being, and how to achieve that, may be the agenda of such an event. Each situation is individual to those enduring it, so the lessons are unique. Rest assured, however, that there is a compassionate lesson within it, if we can shift our perception to be able to see it.

Because abortion revolves around a conscious choice, the impact of this lesson may be greater for those who choose it. They may be balancing karma from previous lifetimes by selecting this option. There may be some important need for psychological, emotional, and spiritual challenge and growth that these people could not experience any other way. Guilt, shame, or intense remorse may be feelings they wished to experience in this lifetime as one of their larger spiritual lessons, and this was the life event that allowed them to challenge their morals and beliefs to work toward a deeper spiritual understanding. I don't think it's right to judge the choices anyone makes, because we never know what that particular soul is trying to achieve in his or her lifetime. We don't have to like the choices, but we have to acknowledge the individual's free will and right to make them.

Do you ever see death in a reading? Can you tell me when I'm going to die? What about my sister, who has been diagnosed with breast cancer?
Before I answer this question, let me relate a story that one of my students shared during a class I taught. She told us that her mother had consulted an astrologer in her younger days, and this astrologer had told her that she would die during a particular astrological event. (I'm not an astrologer, so I can't remember the event, but it was one that occurred annually.) Every year, when that astrological event loomed on the horizon, my student's mom would grow worried and upset, wondering if this was her year to pass into Spirit. When this lady finally did make her transition, guess what? It wasn't during that astrological event! This poor woman spent many years fretting about whether or not she was going to die (and, let's face it—we're *all* going to die someday) instead of enjoying her life and the days she had in it. Is that really how you want to live?

Spirit has never shown me death in a reading, perhaps because it's a hard and fast rule I've made. I don't wish to see when people are going to die, including my loved ones and me, because I don't think it's necessary information to have. In fact, I think it could be quite dangerous to my own mental health and happiness. I honestly cannot see any positive reason why someone would want to know when he's going to pass, especially when you consider the ramifications of charting specific lessons in a lifetime. I've had people ask me about death in readings, and I simply say, "Sorry. You're asking the wrong medium, because Spirit doesn't show death to me." End of conversation.

As for someone diagnosed with a terminal disease: I am a true believer in the power of healing and prayer. I've seen miraculous healings take place for people with terminal illnesses, and I've seen folks pass away after prayers and healing have been offered and done for them. Keep in mind that for many suffering from pain, death is the ultimate healing. There are no afflictions or discomfort on the Other Side, and life continues on as pure energy, surrounded by beauty, peace, and incredible love. If we can begin to see death as a mere transition to a wonderful home, perhaps we can remove our fear of it, thus living our life here to the fullest by realizing our greatest potential.

Why can't you get the winning lottery numbers for me in a reading?

Apparently because you didn't chart it in your life to win the lottery! Honestly—I always chuckle when I hear this question, because when you think about it, where are the life lessons that challenge us to learn if everything is handed to us without us making any effort? Many people believe that winning the lottery, or just being a wealthy individual, will solve all of their problems. However, I can guarantee that the rich people on this Earth have their own sets of issues and life lessons they're trying to learn, which aren't necessarily any easier than yours or mine.

Wealth does not equate with happiness—just look at the story of Siddhartha Gautama. Born as a prince and secluded in a lavish lifestyle for nearly three decades, he finally ventured outside his palace and was stunned to see the suffering of those around him. Disillusioned, he left his wife, child, and luxurious home the next day to try to find a way to end suffering. For the next several years, he undertook rigorous study and disciplined meditation, only to find that this extreme lifestyle was not the way to happiness, any more than the life he'd led as a prince. When he made this realization, he sat to meditate, clearing his mind of all distractions, and that day he was enlightened. At the age of thirty-five, Siddhartha Gautama became the Buddha, the Enlightened One, and devoted the rest of his life to helping others achieve their own spiritual best. If money were the root of all happiness, the Buddha would never have stepped outside his own reality to search for something more.

If you're concerned about prosperity, change your thinking. The Universe is abundance; humanity, however, sees and affirms lack, which draws more of it to us. Try asserting your own abundance and prosperity by saying affirmations every day, such as "My life is filled with abundance and wealth" or "I have enough money to meet all of my needs, and more." You'll be amazed at what energy you attract when you move out of a mindset of deficiency and into one of prosperity.

I want to honor my deceased loved ones. What should I do?

You must find something that resonates for you. Many people honor their loved ones by visiting the cemetery where they're buried. Some folks plant a tree in the loved one's memory or donate money to a worthy charity in the name of the person who has passed. If your loved one left a piece of jewelry or artwork to you, perhaps wearing it or displaying it in your home is an appropriate way to honor her. If you're a writer, maybe you'd like to pen a tribute to your loved one, or if you're an artist, perhaps you could paint a picture to represent the relationship the two of you shared. Find something that's meaningful to both you and the person you wish to remember, and I know you'll honor your loved one in the best way possible.

I like to do simple things to honor those who have passed from my life. My mother's death had the greatest impact on me, and I still miss her every day. There is a framed picture of her on my personal altar in my bedroom, and I often wear her wedding rings, which she wanted me to have when she died. I occasionally visit her gravesite, usually on her birthday and on the day she passed (which is very close to Mother's Day) to leave flowers. I don't spend a lot of time at the cemetery, however, because I know my mother is always around me. I know she can hear me when I think of her, and I know she's never really left me. These thoughts bring me a great deal of comfort. Still, I do honor her by wearing her jewelry, by telling people about her, and by holding her memories close in my heart. And I know I'll see her again.

How can I honor my spirit guides for working with me?

Before I say anything else, I have to tell you this: as honored as you are to work with Spirit, your guides are just as honored to work with you. Many people become uncomfortable when I mention this, but your spirit guides love you so much and truly celebrate the opportunity to serve you. Remember that as you advance, your spirit teachers advance as well, so your relationship is mutually beneficial. The love your guides bring to you is an incredible source of strength and blessing.

To honor my guides, I often keep mementos around that connect me to them. My joy guide, Mara, loves the song "You Are My Sunshine," so I have several knickknacks that display those words in a colorful way. I have many wizard objects, including a stuffed doll and a lovely pewter pin, that remind me of my master guide, Merlin. I have several Native American items that hold energy for my shaman, Black Hawk, and I collect Arthurian memorabilia that connects me to my protector guide, Arthur. Even the Archangel Metatron is a constant presence in my home thanks to a painting I commissioned from my friend, a spirit artist who captured his energy in the work she produced. These are just some examples of how you could honor your guides; I'm sure if you meditate with them, they'll help you think of some lovely ways to keep their presences at the forefront of your mind.

What is a portal? How do you know if there's one in your home?

Metaphysicians believe that a portal is a large opening or gateway into other dimensions and realms of Spirit. Many believe these portals populate areas sacred to early native and magickal traditions because these practitioners intuitively chose these natural spaces due to the spirit energy prevalent there. Portals still exist today, and some esoteric thinkers seek them out, trying to find doorways to other worlds.

Although many portals tend to be outdoors, I wouldn't rule out the possibility of an indoor portal or one that exists inside a person's home. It may be that someone chose to build a house on the portal after sensing the incredible energy of the place. I also believe that you can create a portal between the worlds by regular use of a space for spirit work and concentration on making the veil between the worlds thinner there, so that spirits can step through it more easily and with more perceivable success.

Spiritualist churches are a good example of this. Over the years that my church has been in a specific place, I sense that a doorway has been created between the worlds that the spirit people know and recognize now, which makes it easier for them to come through and be present to deliver their messages to our congregation. Having served at Inspiration Stump in Lily Dale, New York, which is the largest Spiritualist center in the United States, I can honestly say that I think a powerful portal has been created in that outdoor venue because of the constant connection with Spirit that has been maintained there for well over a century. I'm sure there are other portals in many places, especially if effort on maintaining the connection to Spirit is given.

Some people believe that mirrors are portals to other worlds. I was introduced to this concept recently when taking a crystal-healing class with a teacher in my area. This gentleman and his wife, who regularly did crystal healings in their home office, had an ornate mirror set up in their healing room. When he invited me to gaze into it, I got the distinct impression that someone was staring back at me, and I don't mean my own reflection!

These healers had discovered that this mirror was a portal to another dimension, guarded by an entity that kept negative spirits from moving through the mirror into our reality. Whenever this couple encountered lower energies around their healing clients, they sent those energies into the mirror, where the guardian would keep them, blocking their way back to this plane and thus helping their clients to clear their energies.

Since then, I've been very interested in setting up my own portal mirror and asking for a positive spirit energy to help me maintain it. I haven't achieved this yet, but my intentions are good! The important thing to remember here is, again, the Law of Attraction. If you produce good energy and maintain a high, loving, positive attitude, nothing evil or negative is going to come through any mirror or portal to affect you. Keep your mind free of fear and your heart filled with hope and love. This will sustain you in all you do.

What does Spirit say about the end of the world?

It seems that some people are worried about how long the Earth will last and if human beings will continue to inhabit it. War and global climate changes have some frightened, while others cling to the fire-and-brimstone warnings of annihilation and Armageddon highlighted in a zealous religious upbringing. No matter what, I don't think anyone wants to watch loved ones suffer or die in agony. While many people fear death, I think most are afraid of a violent one. That's enough to make anyone wonder what the ultimate end of the world as we know it will bring.

Spirit is eternal. There is an afterlife, and our souls continue on in other planes, in worlds very like this one but free of the worry, frustration, and pain we so often encounter here. Because those planes are filled with the loving, compassionate energy of Creator, my sense of this world's end is not permeated by violence or fear but instead by positive, uplifting Light. If we all go out together at once, it seems logical that we would be taken without pain, just as we are taken individually from our bodies to become once again the unfettered spirits we've always been.

When I pose this question to my own spirit guides, my master teacher, Merlin, impresses upon me the importance of stewardship of this planet. He makes me feel that we don't have to expect a day when the entire population of human beings will be swept up into Spirit, even if it's a positive experience. If we maintain what's been given to us—the seas, the sky, the vegetation, the other creatures of the world—then we can continue this existence for many, many more years, allowing our souls to keep coming here to experience the myriad lessons that are available to us for our spiritual progression. Yes, we can progress in the spirit planes, too—but progress here is so much more meaningful and advances us more deeply than we can understand.

It's another one of those free-will decisions we all need to make collectively: we can take care of this planet, and each other, and continue to exist for a very long time, or we can ignore the needs of our natural world and our brothers and sisters, thus shortening our timeline. It's all up to us.

CONCLUSION

It all started with a question, didn't it?

You must have picked up this book because you had a question, or maybe several, about Spirit, and you hoped that you might find some answers. Perhaps now, that hope has been fulfilled. My goal in writing this book was to provide as many answers as I could to any reader who sought them. I feel pretty good about holding up my end of the bargain.

But it can't stop here. The famous Greek philosopher and teacher Socrates encouraged his followers to engage in strenuous debates using a questioning technique intended to force the seeker to explore others' positions, promote rational thinking, and find ideas worthy of further analysis. The best teachers want their students to continue to investigate, to reach beyond the confines of what has come before, and to discover new, uncharted territories of thought. This, my friends, is my challenge to you.

And you're not alone if you decide to take it up. Your spirit guides, teachers, angels, and loved ones who dwell in the spirit world are ready, willing, and able to help you scout hidden avenues and shed light into darkened areas that haven't yet been explored. All you need is your curiosity, your open mind and heart, and your intention to work within a loving vibration as you delve into the mysteries of Spirit. From my own experience, I can tell you that you'll be amazed by the rewards that flow into every aspect of your life.

And so, dear reader and fellow Seeker of the Light, I thank you for traveling with me through the realms of Spirit. I'm grateful to have been a small part of your adventure. I leave you with this thought, from the great writer Leo Tolstoy: "Life consists in penetrating the unknown, and fashioning our actions in accord with the new knowledge thus acquired."

May knowledge flow to you, may life unfold in all its beauty and mystery, and may your soul rejoice in its journey toward enlightenment.

APPENDIX

The following meditations are recommended for beginners and can be read into a recording device to be played back over headphones. When reading the script, use a calm, gentle, slow voice. Pauses are indicated (. . .) in the scripts. To begin a meditation experience, clear your space of distractions. Sit in a comfortable chair with your feet flat on the floor and your spine straight. Close your eyes and listen to your guided meditation. Concentrate on the voice you are hearing. If you find yourself falling asleep, sit on the edge of your chair to remind your mind to stay focused.

WHITE LIGHT MEDITATION

*This meditation is recommended to begin your day in
a positive way. It should also be done before any spirit*

communication is initiated. (This script can be used in conjunction with other meditative experiences. Begin with the White Light Meditation and then add onto it any other guided scripts you wish.)

Close your eyes and relax. Listen to the sound of my voice. Take a deep breath . . . hold it . . . and let it out slowly. Take another deep breath . . . hold it . . . and release it. Another deep breath in . . . hold it . . . and let it out.

As you continue breathing in . . . breathing out . . . you become more and more relaxed. Breathe in . . . positive light energy. Breathe out . . . negative thoughts and feelings. Inhale . . . love and relaxation. Exhale . . . pain and worry. Every breath takes you to a deeper state of relaxation.

You feel your body relaxing . . . your feet relax, melting into the floor . . . Your legs relax, all tension flowing out of them . . . Your hips and lower back relax, your body sinking deeper into the chair . . . Your hands and arms relax, all stress flowing out of them through your fingertips . . . Your abdomen and chest relax, feeling heavier and softer . . . Your neck and shoulders relax, all tension draining out of them . . . Your jaw and face relax, become softer . . .

You are more relaxed, more at peace, more centered, more balanced. Every breath takes you deeper. Ever sound in the room only serves to take you deeper. Stray thoughts that come in simply skitter away, taking you deeper into relaxation. You feel safe and balanced, relaxed and at peace . . .

Now, in this lovely relaxed state, look within your body, looking with your mind's eye into the very core of your being.

You see into the center of your body, in your solar plexus, the area just above your navel. You look here, and you notice a pinprick of light, a tiny spark in the center of your being. You understand immediately that this is your Divine Spark, the Light of Creator within you, and you feel immensely happy as you realize this.

As you watch, this tiny light begins to grow bigger and brighter. The light gets bigger . . . bigger . . . bigger . . . filling up your entire body with beautiful, bright White Light. This beautiful Light continues to fill you up, filling your torso . . . filling your legs and feet . . . filling your arms and hands . . . filling your neck and head . . . until your entire body is consumed by this beautiful, bright White Light of Creator. You shine—bright, beautiful, joyful, relaxed, and at peace, a lovely Beacon of Divine Light.

Now, as you watch, the White Light shining within you expands outside of your body, encircling you in a beautiful egg of Light. All around you, the Light encompasses you . . . above your head . . . below your feet . . . on every side . . . You feel safe and protected in this Light, and you know that only good and positive energy can reach you as you stand in Creator's Light. And as you *are* Creator's Light, you know that only positive energy can go forth from you. Only love surrounds you and manifests within you . . . only love touches you. You are safe, protected, and loved beyond measure.

Now, take several minutes to enjoy the beautiful White Light of Creator. It surrounds you and penetrates you. It brings love and positive energy to you. Nothing but good can come to you, and nothing but good can go from you as you dwell constantly in this Light. Enjoy the feeling . . . know how safe and loved you are. If any stray thoughts come into your mind, simply acknowledge them and release them into the Light. Continue to enjoy the Divine Presence of the Light.

* (*Pause for several minutes. If you wish to add any other guided meditation script prompts, here is the place to put them.*)

And now it is time to begin to come back to the physical world . . . but as you come back, you bring with you the beautiful, loving Light of Creator. It still shines within from the very core of your being, attracting to it only positive, loving vibrations. You remain a Divine Being, for you remain in the Light of the Divine. The Light within you is never extinguished . . . you carry it with you always, wherever you go.

** So now begin to come back to the physical reality around you . . . begin to feel your body once again . . . begin to feel the ground beneath your feet . . . the chair underneath you. Begin to wiggle your fingers and toes . . . slowly become aware of the sounds of the room around you. Slowly, you move in your chair, coming back to full awareness of the physical world. And when you're ready . . . open your eyes, wide awake and relaxed . . . wide awake and at peace.

Spirit Connection Meditation

Begin this meditation by going through the entire White Light Meditation up to the *. Once there, add this meditation script to connect with your guides, teachers, or loved ones in the spirit world.

Now, as you watch, the circle of White Light continues to expand all around you on every side. As it expands, you notice several figures standing within the Light. You know immediately that these are your spirit guides, teachers, angels, and loved ones, and you are happy to see them here in this space between the worlds. All of them are present because they love you and wish to connect with you. You can take time to connect with each of them in turn, or perhaps you wish to connect with a particular spirit today. If you think of one, that spirit will approach you. If there is no particular spirit you wish to consult, the one you most need to connect with today will approach you. You watch as this happens, and your heart is filled with joyful anticipation as the spirit comes forward to greet you . . .

Notice everything about the spirit that comes forward. See how the spirit looks . . . hear the voice in your mind . . . feel the warmth of the embrace . . . This spirit loves you more than you can possibly know, and you can sense the depth of that love as it emanates from your spirit loved one.

Take some time now to commune with your spirit friend. Ask any questions you wish, and be sure to listen to any messages the spirit has to impart to you. Know that you will remember everything that transpires in this communication, so enjoy your contact without boundaries. Do this now.

(*Long pause of three to five minutes.*)

And now, it is time for you to take your leave from this place between the worlds to return fully to the physical plane. Know, however, that your spirit friends are close about you at all times, and you need merely to think of them and they will be immediately accessible to you. Know too that you will remember everything that happened during this experience, and you will understand it all when you have time to recall it.

(*Go now to the ** in the White Light Meditation to bring yourself back to the physical world.*)

⌒

After all meditation experiences, it's a good idea to write down your memories and impressions so that you can look back upon them at a later time. Jot down everything you remember, especially if you feel you received guidance to questions that you asked. You'll be amazed to discover answers as you meditate more and more with your spirit loved ones. You may also want to eat or drink something after a meditation experience to further ground your energy back in the physical world.

Acknowledgments

As usual, I have many people to thank for their assistance with this project. The following folks submitted questions expressly for the manuscript, and I extend to them my sincere appreciation:

Adele Armstrong, Michelle Cooper, Mary Lynn Crawford, Larry Davis, Tawnya Fletcher, Jay B. Fox, Kim Frey, Sara Gerhardt, Kathy Glasgow, Brenda Goetz, Sara Hensley, Monica Hirth, Sally Kurz, Mary Kurnick Maass, Shawna Mahan, Holly McCullough, Donna Mueller, Cindy Mullen, Irene Olivier, Nick Reiter, Bev Riley, Vicki Romito, Suzanne Sagrati, Travis Sanders, Linda Simonsen, Kate Strong, Michelle Wisbith, and Sue Yokitis.

I also wish to acknowledge the following for their help with specific examples and for sharing their knowledge and experiences with me:

Candy Bloise, Gwynne Gabbard, Lori Leach, Donna Honeycutt and Lynne Ford, Gene and Barbara Jackson, and Michelle and Sam Wisbith.

Extra-special thanks to Reverend Joanne Franchina, for books galore, and to Reverend Jaccolin Franchina, for important insights into past lives.

Sincere and abundant gratitude to my band of spirit helpers: Mara, Merlin, Arthur, Black Hawk, Dr. Wilkins, Messiel, and Archangel Metatron. None of this could be done without you; thank you for traveling with me in this lifetime.

Finally, to the closest members of my soul group, Max, Ben, and especially Keith: you'll never realize what you bring to me every day through your presence in my life. "I love you" just doesn't suffice . . . but I do.

REFERENCES

Barker, Elsa. *Letters from the Afterlife*: *A Guide to the Other Side.* Hillsboro, OR: Beyond Words, 1995.

"Bodhicitta" (username). "Buddhists—Guardian or Forces and Spirit Guides." *AllExperts.com*, December 20, 2004. http://en.allexperts.com/q/Buddhists-948/Guardian-forces-spirit-guides.htm (accessed February 24, 2009).

Browne, Sylvia, with Lindsay Harrison. *Life on the Other Side: A Psychic's Tour of the Afterlife.* New York: Dutton, 2000.

Chopra, Deepak. *Life After Death: The Burden of Proof.* 2006. New York: Harmony Books, 2006.

Dennis, Geoffrey. "Maggid: Jewish Spirit Guide, Revealing Angel," *Jewish Myth, Magic, and Mysticism* blog, September 2, 2007. http://ejmmm2007.blogspot.com/2007/09/

maggid-jewish-spirit-guide-revealing.html (accessed February 24, 2009).

FAQs.org. "Question 12.22: What Is the Jewish Position on Communicating with the Dead?" http://www.faqs.org/faqs/judaism/FAQ/06-Jewish-Thought/section-23.html (accessed February 24, 2009).

Garvey, Mark. *Searching for Mary: An Exploration of Marian Apparitions Across the U.S.* New York: Plume, 1998.

Global Oneness. "Hinduism and Death." http://www.experiencefestival.com/a/Hinduismand_Death/id/54141 (accessed January 23, 2009).

Good News Bible: Today's English Version. Second edition. New York: Thomas Nelson Publishers, 1992.

Gudzune, Jeffrey R. "Talking with Spirits: Communication with the Dead to Help the Living." *Suite101.com*, May 5, 2008. http://nativeamericanfirstnationshistory.suite101.com/article.cfm/talking_with_spirits (accessed February 24, 2009).

Guggenheim, Bill, and Judy Guggenheim. *Hello from Heaven!* New York: Bantam, 1995.

Kessinger, Thomas A. "Genesis of Catholic Schools in Southwestern Ohio," 2008. http://www.allacademic.com//meta/p_mla_apa_research_citation/2/7/3/8/0/pages273805/p273805-1.php (accessed August 31, 2009).

Klingler, Sharon Anne. *Advanced Spirit Communication and Public Mediumship.* Second edition. Westlake, OH: Starbringer Press, 2008.

Kübler-Ross, Elisabeth. *On Death and Dying.* New York: Simon and Schuster, 1969.

Matheson, Richard. *What Dreams May Come.* New York: Tor, 1978.

Moody, Raymond A., Jr. *Life After Life.* New York: Harper-Collins, 2001.

Newton, Michael. *Journey of Souls: Case Studies of Life Between Lives.* St. Paul, MN: Llewellyn, 1994.

Robinson, B. A., and Ontario Consultants on Religious Tolerance. "Religions of the World: Shinto." *Religious Tolerance.org,* December 14, 2007. http://www.religious tolerance.org/shinto.htm (accessed February 24, 2009).

———. "Demonic Possession & Oppression; Exorcism." *ReligiousTolerance.org,* November 30, 2006. http://www .religioustolerance.org/chr_exor9.htm (accessed March 16, 2009).

Sakellarios, Stephen. "Reincarnation in Beliefs." *AllExperts .com,* February 2, 2005. http://en.allexperts.com/q/ Reincarnation-3284/Reincarnation-Beliefs.htm (accessed March 3, 2009).

Schindler, William. "Hindus—Personal Guardian Angels or Forces and Spirit Guides." *AllExperts.com,* December 20, 2004. http://en.allexperts.com/q/Hindus-946/ personal-Guardian-Angels-forces.htm (accessed February 24, 2009).

Schwartz, Gary E. *The Afterlife Experiments: Breakthrough Scientific Evidence of Life After Death.* New York: Pocket Books, 2002.

Segal, Eliezer. "In Seventh Heaven." http://www.ucalgary
.ca/~elsegal/Shokel/891103_7th_Heaven.html (accessed
January 23, 2009).

Taylor, Troy. "Hauntings: Poltergeist-Like Activity," 2004.
http://www.prairieghosts.com/polter.html (accessed March
16, 2009).

Tucker, Jim B. *Life Before Life: A Scientific Investigation of
Children's Memories of Previous Lives.* New York: St. Mar-
tin's Press, 2005.

Vanden Eynden, Rose. *So You Want to Be a Medium? A Down-
to-Earth Guide.* Woodbury, MN: Llewellyn, 2006.

Weiss, Brian L. *Many Lives, Many Masters: The True Story of a
Prominent Psychiatrist, His Young Patient, and the Past-Life
Therapy That Changed Both Their Lives.* New York: Fire-
side, 1988.

White Eagle. *Spiritual Unfoldment 1.* Liss, England: White
Eagle Publishing Trust, 1961.

Free Catalog

Get the latest information on our body, mind, and spirit products! To receive a **free** copy of Llewellyn's consumer catalog, *New Worlds of Mind & Spirit,* simply call 1-877-NEW-WRLD or visit our website at www.llewellyn.com and click on *New Worlds.*

☾ LLEWELLYN ORDERING INFORMATION

Order Online:
Visit our website at www.llewellyn.com, select your books, and order them on our secure server.

Order by Phone:
- Call toll-free within the U.S. at 1-877-NEW-WRLD (1-877-639-9753). Call toll-free within Canada at 1-866-NEW-WRLD (1-866-639-9753)
- We accept VISA, MasterCard, and American Express

Order by Mail:
Send the full price of your order (MN residents add 6.875% sales tax) in U.S. funds, plus postage & handling to:

> **Llewellyn Worldwide**
> **2143 Wooddale Drive, Dept. 978-0-7387-1898-9**
> **Woodbury, MN 55125-2989**

Postage & Handling:
Standard (U.S., Mexico & Canada). If your order is:
$24.99 and under, add $4.00
$25.00 and over, FREE STANDARD SHIPPING

AK, HI, PR: $16.00 for one book plus $2.00 for each additional book.

International Orders (airmail only):
$16.00 for one book plus $3.00 for each additional book

Orders are processed within 2 business days.
Please allow for normal shipping time. Postage and handling rates subject to change.

So You Want to Be a Medium?

A Down-to-Earth Guide

ROSE VANDEN EYNDEN

Are you fascinated by the spirit world? Wish you could communicate with loved ones on the Other Side? According to Spiritualist minister Rose Vanden Eynden, everyone possesses innate capabilities for spirit communication. Emphasizing the principles of modern Spiritualism, *So You Want to Be a Medium?* demonstrates how to enhance one's spiritual senses for working between worlds.

Through exercises involving meditation, breathing, dream work, symbols, and energy systems, the author teaches how to prepare one's mind and body for spiritual communication. Readers also learn about the many kinds of spirit guides and elemental energies, how to get in touch with them, and how to interpret their messages. Whether you're seeking to become a professional medium or simply interested in a closer connection to the Creator, this fascinating guide to the spirit world can enrich your spiritual life—no matter what your religious background.

978-0-7387-0856-0, 288 pp., 6 x 9   **$14.95**

Metatron

Invoking the Angel of God's Presence

Rose Vanden Eynden

With Metatron in your corner, you're only a petition away from a better life. Rose Vanden Eynden may be the first to devote an entire book to this powerful celestial being—revealing his unique place in the angelic realm and demonstrating how to connect with this wise and compassionate archangel.

Metatron's close proximity to the Creator and connection to humanity make him the ideal angelic ally. Representing balance and unity, this angelic force can help in all areas of personal development. You'll also discover how to contact the "Angel of the Presence" through meditation, dreamwork, ritual, and inspirational writing. There are specific ceremonies for building a closer relationship with the Creator, healing on a global scale, balancing masculine and feminine energies, material/spiritual pursuits, and karmic issues.

Also featured is an insightful Q and A with Metatron, channeled by the author to answer compelling questions on life, death, faith, and spirit.

978-0-7387-1343-4, 240 pp., 5³⁄₁₆ x 8   **$13.95**